Apress Pocket Guides

Apress Pocket Guides present concise summaries of cutting-edge developments and working practices throughout the tech industry. Shorter in length, books in this series aims to deliver quick-to-read guides that are easy to absorb, perfect for the time-poor professional.

This series covers the full spectrum of topics relevant to the modern industry, from security, AI, machine learning, cloud computing, web development, product design, to programming techniques and business topics too.

Typical topics might include:

- A concise guide to a particular topic, method, function or framework

- Professional best practices and industry trends

- A snapshot of a hot or emerging topic

- Industry case studies

- Concise presentations of core concepts suited for students and those interested in entering the tech industry

- Short reference guides outlining 'need-to-know' concepts and practices.

More information about this series at https://link.springer.com/bookseries/17385.

Spring Security 6 Recipes

Essential Techniques for Quick and Secure Java Applications

Massimo Nardone

Apress®

Spring Security 6 Recipes: Essential Techniques for Quick and Secure Java Applications

Massimo Nardone
Helsinki, Finland

ISBN-13 (pbk): 979-8-8688-1296-5   ISBN-13 (electronic): 979-8-8688-1297-2
https://doi.org/10.1007/979-8-8688-1297-2

Managing Director, Apress Media LLC: Welmoed Spahr
Acquisitions Editor: Melissa Duffy
Development Editor: Laura Berendson
Editorial Project Manager: Gryffin Winkler

Cover designed by eStudioCalamar

Distributed to the book trade worldwide by Springer Science+Business Media New York, 1 New York Plaza, Suite 4600, New York, NY 10004-1562, USA. Phone 1-800-SPRINGER, fax (201) 348-4505, e-mail orders-ny@springer-sbm.com, or visit www.springeronline.com. Apress Media, LLC is a California LLC and the sole member (owner) is Springer Science + Business Media Finance Inc (SSBM Finance Inc). SSBM Finance Inc is a **Delaware** corporation.

For information on translations, please e-mail booktranslations@springernature.com; for reprint, paperback, or audio rights, please e-mail bookpermissions@springernature.com.

Apress titles may be purchased in bulk for academic, corporate, or promotional use. eBook versions and licenses are also available for most titles. For more information, reference our Print and eBook Bulk Sales web page at http://www.apress.com/bulk-sales.

Any source code or other supplementary material referenced by the author in this book is available to readers on GitHub. For more detailed information, please visit https://www.apress.com/gp/services/source-code.

If disposing of this product, please recycle the paper

This book is dedicated to the memory of my loving late father Giuseppe. Your support, your education, your values made me the man I am now. You will be loved and missed forever. I also would like to dedicate this book to my children Luna, Leo and Neve. Your love and support mean everything to me.
—Massimo

Table of Contents

About the Author

 **Massimo Nardone** has more than 29 years of experience in information and cybersecurity for IT/OT/IoT/IIoT, web/mobile development, cloud, and IT architecture. His true IT passions are security and Android. He holds an MSc in computing science from the University of Salerno, Italy. Throughout his working career, he has held various positions, starting as a programming developer and then security teacher, PCI QSA, auditor, assessor, lead IT/OT/SCADA/cloud architect, CISO, BISO, executive, program director, OT/IoT/IIoT security competence leader, VP of OT security, etc. In his last working engagement, he worked as a seasoned cyber and information security executive, CISO, and OT, IoT, and IIoT security competence leader, helping many clients to develop and implement cyber, information, OT, and IoT security activities. He is currently working as Vice President of OT security for SSH Communications Security. He is author of three books such as Secure RESTful APIs, Spring Security 6 Recipes and Cybersecurity in the Gaming Industry. Plus, he is a coauthor of numerous Apress books, including *Pro Spring Security, Pro JPA 2 in Java EE 8*, and *Pro Android Games*, and has reviewed more than 75 titles.

About the Technical Reviewer

 **Mario Faliero** is a telecommunications engineer and entrepreneur. He has more than ten years of experience with radio 1 frequency hardware engineering. Mario has extensive experience in numerical coding, using scripting languages (MATLAB, Python) and compiled languages (C/C++, Java). He has been responsible for the development of electromagnetic assessment tools for space and commercial applications. Mario received his master's degree from the University of Siena.

Acknowledgments

Many thanks go to my wonderful children, Luna, Leo, and Neve, for supporting me all the time. You are and will always be the most beautiful reason of my life.

I want to thank my beloved late father Giuseppe and my mother Maria, who always supported me and loved me so much. I will love and miss both of you forever. My beloved brothers, Roberto and Mario, for your endless love and for being the best brothers in the world. Brunaldo and Kaisa for bringing joy and happiness to Luna and Leo.

Thanks a lot to Melissa Duffy for giving me the opportunity to work as writer on this book, to Shobana Srinivasan for doing such a great job during the editorial process and supporting me all the time, and of course Mario Faliero, the technical reviewer of this book, for helping me to make the book better.

—Massimo

Acknowledgments

Introduction

This book is for Spring Security beginners with a Spring Security 6 and Boot 3–based Java Application Problem-Solution Approach to secure the web tier. It will be a practical pocket guide to help the developers understand how to develop and deploy secure Spring Framework 6 and Spring Boot 3–based Enterprise Java applications with the Spring Security Framework.

It will be structured as a problem and recipes, so for each small or big need there will be a solution provided.

This book is about Spring Framework 6 and Spring Boot 3. It is a tutorial and reference that guides you through the implementation of the security features for a Java Web Application by presenting consistent solutions to security issues with Spring.

This book explores a comprehensive set of functionalities to implement industry-standard authentication and authorization mechanisms for Java applications, providing examples on how to develop customized Spring Security login/logout, Spring Security and two-factor authentication, etc.

To get the most out of this book, we recommend having the Spring Security source code checked out on your computer and working through the examples alongside both the book's content and the Spring Security codebase. This hands-on approach will not only help you grasp each concept as it's introduced but also teach valuable programming techniques and best practices. Whenever possible, this method of studying software is highly effective. If the source code is available, make sure to explore it—sometimes, a few lines of code can convey more than a thousand words.

In this book, we focus on introducing Spring Boot 3, analyzing the Spring Framework, and building Java Web Applications using Spring Security v6 and Java 23. Spring Security v6 supports a wide range of authentication mechanisms, and this book will look into Spring Security 6 integration with H2 DB, JWT, OAuth2.0, etc.

Prerequisites

The examples in this book are all built with Java 17+ and Maven 3.9.9. Spring Security 6 was the version used throughout the book. Tomcat Web Server v11 was used for the different web applications in the book, mainly through its Maven plug-
in, and the laptop used was a ThinkPad Yoga 360 with 8GB of RAM. All the projects were developed using the IntelliJ IDEA Ultimate 2024.2.4.

You are free to use your own tools and operating system. Because everything is Java based, you should be able to compile your programs on any platform without problems.

Downloading the Code

The code for the examples given in this book is available via the Download Source Code button located at `https://github.com/Apress/Spring-Security-6-Recipes`.

CHAPTER 1

Development Tools

This pocketbook is in a problem-solution format, intended for Spring Security beginners with a Spring Security 6 and H2 DB–based Java Application Problem-Solution Approach to secure the web tier.

It is a practical pocket guide to help you understand how to develop and deploy secure Spring Framework 6 and Spring Boot 3–based Enterprise Java applications with the Spring Security Framework and H2 DB.

The chapters of the book have a problem-solution structure, so for each small or big need there will be a solution provided.

In this book, we will explore the comprehensive set of functionalities to implement industry-standard authentication and authorization mechanisms for Java applications, providing examples on how to develop customized Spring Security with JSP tags and Thymeleaf, Boot Initializr, Data JDBC, etc.

What Is Spring Security 6?

Spring Security 6 is the latest version of the **Spring Security** Framework, designed to provide comprehensive security features for Java applications, particularly those built on the **Spring** ecosystem. It focuses on authentication, authorization, and protection against common security vulnerabilities, such as Cross-Site Request Forgery (CSRF) and session fixation attacks.

© Massimo Nardone 2025
M. Nardone, *Spring Security 6 Recipes*, Apress Pocket Guides,
https://doi.org/10.1007/979-8-8688-1297-2_1

Here's an overview of what's new and essential about Spring and what the key features of Spring Security 6 are:

1. **Java 17 and Spring Framework 6+ Compatibility**

   - Spring Security 6 requires **Java 17+** and is built to be compatible with **Spring Framework 6** and **Spring Boot 3**. This enables developers to use the latest language features and performance improvements in Java 17.

2. **Focus on Modern Security Practices**

   - The shift toward **Zero Trust Security** principles, where every request is authenticated and authorized independently, is supported in Spring Security.

3. **Authorization with a Centralized Authorization Manager**

   - Spring Security 6 introduces the **AuthorizationManager API** as a centralized way to manage and configure access control across your application. This provides a unified way to apply authorization rules across different layers and endpoints.

4. **OAuth 2.1 Support**

   - With OAuth 2.0 being widely adopted, Spring Security 6 includes updated support for **OAuth 2.1**.

5. **Security Filter Chain Customization**

   - The configuration process for security filters has been streamlined with the **SecurityFilterChain** bean. This allows more flexible and modular configurations of security rules.

6. **New Authorization and Access Policies**

- Expanded support for custom authorization rules allows developers to define specific access policies for different types of requests and roles with annotations like @PreAuthorize and @PostAuthorize, along with the new AuthorizationManager, so you can define custom rules for each endpoint or service more intuitively.

7. **Enhanced Security Context Management**

- Improvements to the **SecurityContextHolder** make it easier to manage user authentication details throughout the application.

- The updated SecurityContext API allows more robust handling of security contexts in reactive applications, making Spring Security 6 well suited for both traditional and reactive programming models.

8. **Built-In Support for Servlet and Reactive Stacks**

- **Reactive Security**: Spring Security 6 is compatible with reactive programming in **Spring WebFlux**, allowing for efficient, nonblocking security mechanisms for real-time applications.

- **Servlet Stack**: Traditional Spring MVC applications can still use all features, while Spring WebFlux users can benefit from nonblocking reactive support.

9. **Improved CSRF Protection**

- CSRF protection mechanisms have been enhanced and simplified, with more secure defaults for managing CSRF tokens and a simplified API for enabling/disabling CSRF protections as needed.

10. **Easier Configuration for Password Encoding**

- Spring Security 6 improves password management by offering more built-in options for **password encoding** with modern hashing algorithms such as **bcrypt**.

Problem

Where does Spring Security fit in and where and why would you use Spring Security?

Solution

Spring Security is a powerful, versatile framework specifically suited for securing Java applications, particularly those using Spring. Here are some key scenarios where it shines:

1. **Web Security**: Protects against common vulnerabilities like Cross-Site Scripting (XSS), CSRF, and clickjacking.

2. **URL Security**: Provides tools for securing URLs, resource access, and enforcing HTTPS.

3. **JVM Languages**: Works best with Java, Groovy, or Kotlin; it's not compatible with non-JVM languages.

4. **Role-Based Access**: Ideal for applications needing role-based authentication/authorization.

5. **Web App Protection**: Restricts access to web applications, blocking unauthorized users.

6. **Provider Integration**: Supports integrations with LDAP, Active Directory, OpenID, and databases.

7. **Object-Level Security**: Allows fine-grained security with Access Control Lists (ACLs) for specific users.

8. **Nonintrusive**: Configurable via filters, XML, SAOP, and annotations, keeping it modular and separate from core business logic.

9. **Service Layer Security**: Applies security rules consistently across layers, including URLs and methods.

10. **Remember Me**: Enables users to stay logged in across visits.

11. **Certificate-Based Authentication**: Supports X.509 certificates for secure client-server authentication.

12. **View Security**: Controls visibility of page elements based on the user's role.

13. **Advanced Access Rules**: Allows custom rules using Spring Expression Language (SpEL).

14. **HTTP Status Handling**: Automatically translates exceptions into HTTP status codes (e.g., 403 for access denied).

15. **API Security**: Secures REST APIs for external applications.

16. **Lightweight Server Compatibility**: Works in environments lacking full Java EE security support.

17. **Java EE Alternative**: Offers more flexibility and ease of use than Java EE's native security.

18. **Seamless Spring Integration**: Ideal for applications already using Spring, as it leverages existing Spring knowledge and tools.

Problem

Why upgrade to Spring Security 6?

Solution

There are several reasons to update to Spring Security 6. Here are some of the most important:

- **Better Performance**: Since Java 17 and improvements of the Spring Security framework, the applications can benefit from better performance and modern language features.

- **Enhanced Security**: Spring Security 6 includes robust, modern security practices that address today's cybersecurity challenges, like Zero Trust and OAuth 2.1.

- **Future-Proofing**: As Spring Framework and Java evolve, older versions of Spring Security may become unsupported. Upgrading to Spring Security 6 ensures compatibility with future Spring and Java releases.

- **Easier Configuration and Customization**: The new AuthorizationManager API and other configuration improvements make it easier to set up fine-grained access control policies without complex configurations.

Let's now set up our development environment.

Setting up an environment for **Spring Security 6** involves configuring dependencies, establishing the appropriate Java version, and setting up a project structure. Spring Security 6 requires Java 17+ and Spring Boot 3, so ensure your environment meets these requirements.

Problem

In setting up the development environment, what is the list of software you'll need to download and install?

Solution

For this book, I used Windows 11 as OS. For our development environment, you need to download and install the following tools in the given order:

- Java SE Development Kit (JDK) 17+ (I used v23 as it was the latest version available)

- IntelliJ IDEA Ultimate Edition 2024.2.4

- Maven 3.9.9

- Apache Tomcat Server v11 (External)

Let's go through the steps required to set up everything properly.

Problem

What is the correct version of the Java SE Development Kit and how to set it up?

Solution

On most operating systems, the JDK comes in an installer or package, so there shouldn't be any problems.

Note   Remember that the Java SE Development Kit and Java SE Runtime Environment (JRE) require at a minimum a Pentium II 266MHz processor, 128MB of memory, and 181MB disk for development tools for 64-bit platforms.

Download the JDK version specific to your Windows operating system from the following link:

`https://www.oracle.com/java/technologies/downloads/#jdk23-windows.`

We will use the JDK version 23.0.1 in this book. Which I have installed on a Windows 11 machine. In my case, I ran the file named "jdk-23_windows-x64_bin.exe" which installed the JDK v23 onto my Windows machine, as shown in Figure 1-1.

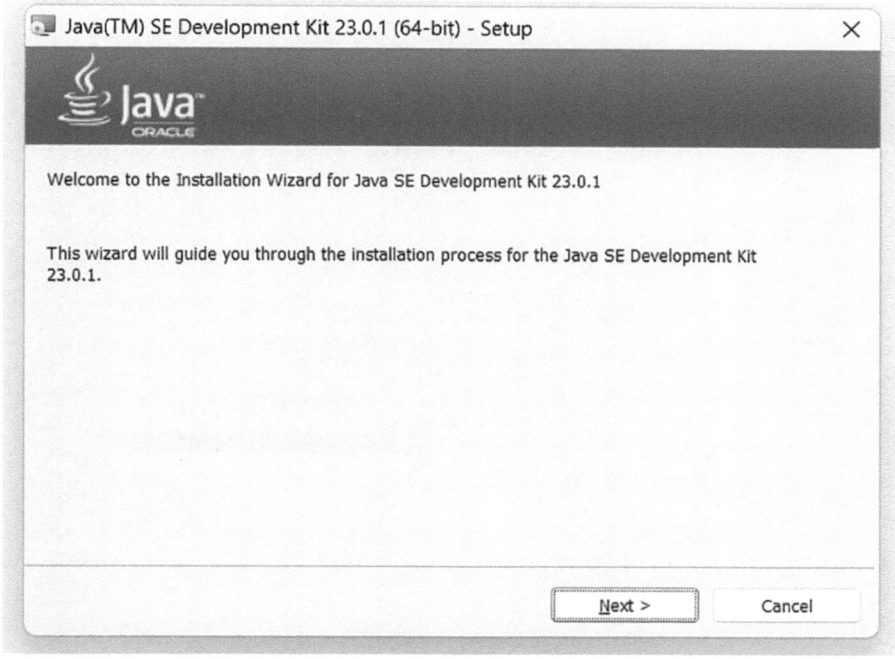

Figure 1-1. *Installing JDK v23*

Let's set a JAVA_HOME system variable by following these steps:

1. Open the Windows Environment Variables.

2. Add the JAVA_HOME variable and point it to the JDK installed folder (in my case, C:\Program Files\ Java\ jdk-23).

3. Append %JAVA_HOME%\bin to the system PATH variable so that all of the Java commands will be accessible from everywhere.

The result is shown in Figure 1-2.

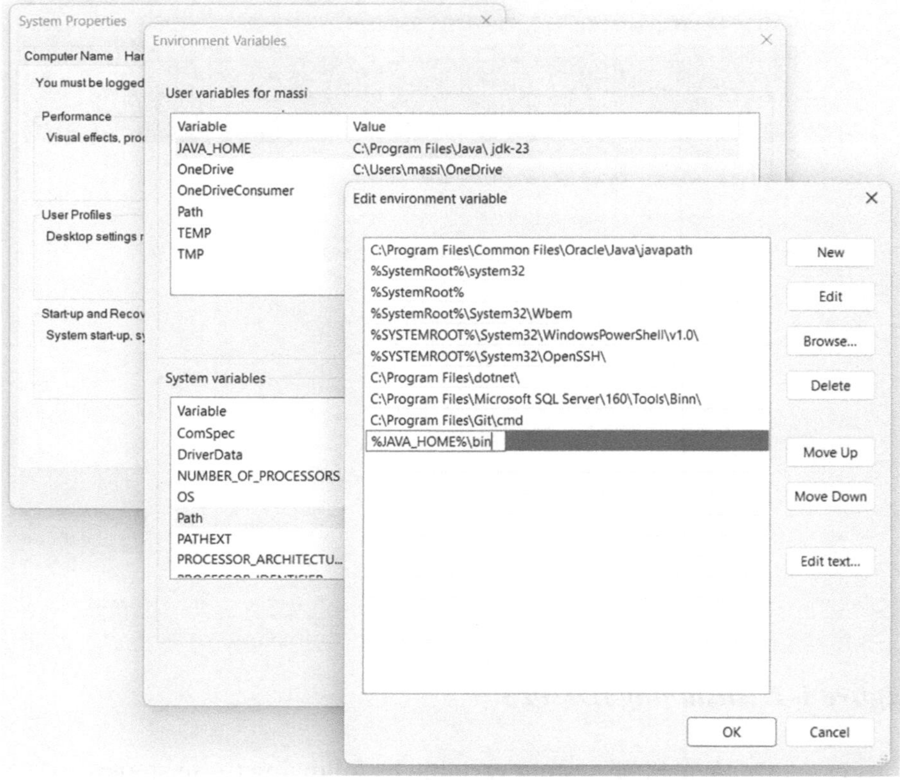

Figure 1-2. *Setting up the JAVA_HOME system variable*

Let's test if the JDK installation was successful. Open a command prompt and type the code shown in Figure 1-3.

Figure 1-3. *Testing the Java installation*

Great! Java is now installed and ready to be used for the examples in the book.

Problem

When using Spring Security v6, you can of course decide freely which integrated development environment (IDE) tool you wish to use.

What is the right IDE to install when developing with Spring Security v6 and why?

Solution

There are mainly two major IDEA commonly used when developing with Spring Security v6, which are

- **IntelliJ IDEA (recommended):** Offers excellent support for Spring projects, with features like Spring Boot support, automatic code completion, Spring Security–specific inspections, and built-in support for JPA, testing, and more.

- **Eclipse with Spring Tools 4 (STS4):** If you prefer Eclipse, install the Spring Tools 4 plug-in for optimized support for Spring applications.

As you can see, IntelliJ IDEA is recommended because in addition to being an excellent support for Spring projects, it also offers features like Spring Boot support and automatic code completion. The main difference is that Eclipse is free of charge, while IntelliJ IDEA is not.

For this book, I used the IntelliJ IDEA Ultimate Edition 2024.2.4, which has a free 30-day trial.

Problem

How to install and configure IntelliJ IDEA Ultimate Edition 2024.2.4?

Solution

You can install the IntelliJ IDEA Ultimate Edition 2024.2.4 for web and enterprise development by following these steps:

1. Download the `.exe` file from `https://www.`
   `jetbrains.com/idea/download/?var=1&section`
   `=windows#section=windows.`

2. Install the `.exe` file, which in our case is named
   `ideaIU-2024.2.4.exe.`

Once installed, the directory should look like Figure 1-4.

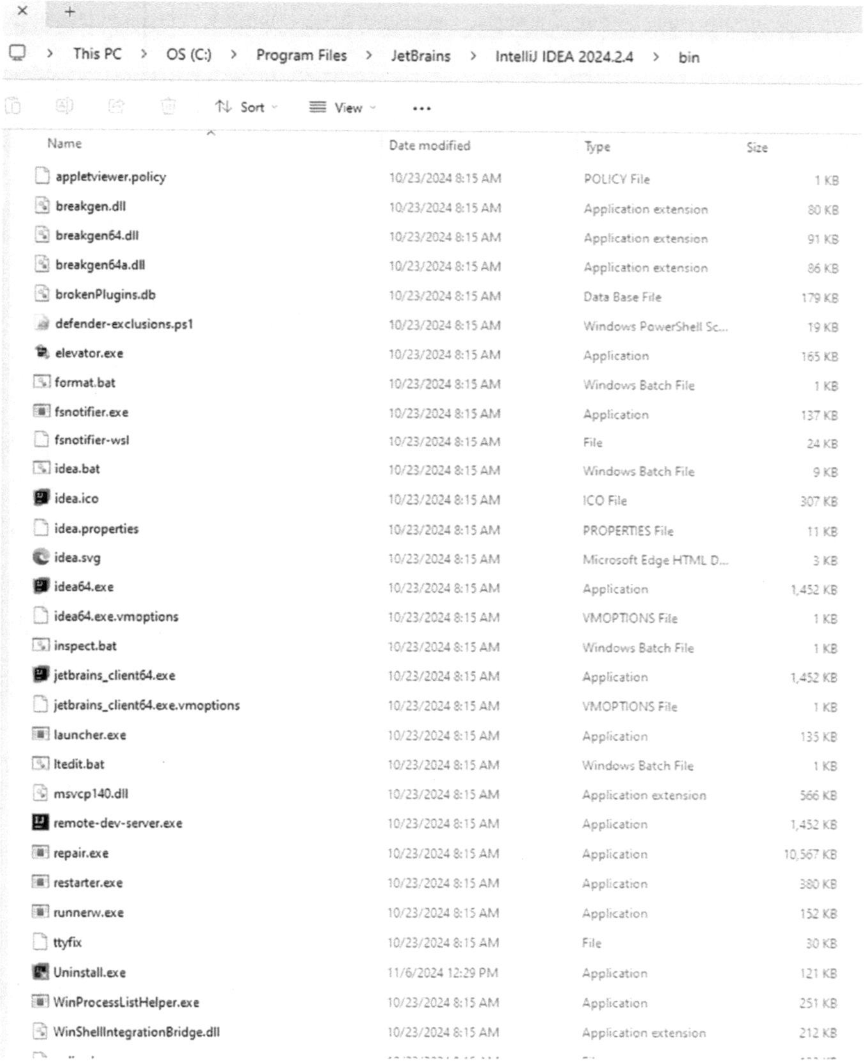

Figure 1-4. *The IntelliJ IDEA 2024.2.4 directory*

Now IntelliJ IDEA Ultimate Edition 2024.2.4 for web and enterprise development tool is ready to be used. Figure 1-5 shows how the dashboard looks when executing it.

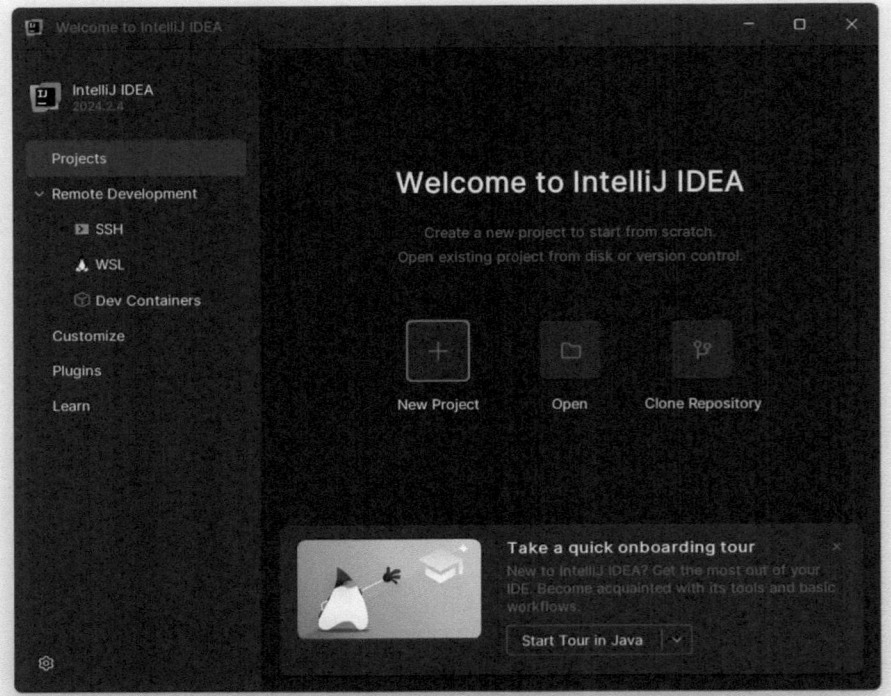

Figure 1-5. *The IntelliJ IDEA Ultimate Edition 2024.2.4 for web and enterprise development dashboard*

Problem

Which build tools should you use when developing with Spring Security v6 and why?

Solution

When developing with **Spring Security 6**, the two most popular build tools you might choose are **Maven** and **Gradle**.

Both tools can manage Spring Security 6's dependencies and build tasks effectively, so the best choice depends on your project and team needs. Many developers start with Maven for simpler projects or if their team has more experience with it and move to Gradle if they require more build optimization and customization.

Why Use Maven?

- **Standardization**: Maven has been around longer and follows a standardized convention-over-configuration approach, which simplifies project structure. This is beneficial if you're working on a team or in an environment that values consistency.

- **Dependency Management**: Maven's dependency management is robust and straightforward. Spring Security 6 depends on Spring Framework 6 and other libraries, which Maven can manage efficiently.

- **Comprehensive Documentation and Community Support**: Since Maven has been widely used in Java projects for many years, there's extensive documentation and community support available, making it easier to find solutions for common issues.

- **Built-In Life Cycle:** Maven provides a default life cycle (such as clean, compile, test, package, and install) that helps structure the build and deployment process without additional configuration.

- **Compatibility with IDEs**: Maven is well supported by all major IDEs, including IntelliJ IDEA, Eclipse, and VS Code, which makes integration with your development environment seamless.

Here is an XML example Maven configuration for Spring Security 6:

```
<dependencies>
    <dependency>
        <groupId>org.springframework.boot</groupId>
        <artifactId>spring-boot-starter-security</artifactId>
    </dependency>
    <dependency>
        <groupId>org.springframework.boot</groupId>
        <artifactId>spring-boot-starter-web</artifactId>
    </dependency>
</dependencies>
```

Problem

Why instead should we use Gradle as a build tool?

Solution

Here are the reasons why to choose Gradle instead of Maven:

- **Flexibility and Performance**: Gradle's build scripts use a Groovy or Kotlin DSL, which provides greater flexibility and conciseness compared to XML-based Maven scripts. Gradle's incremental build system often leads to faster builds, which is particularly useful for larger projects.

- **Easier Customization**: Gradle's script-based approach makes it easy to customize the build process. You can create custom tasks and automate complex build logic that might be challenging to achieve with Maven.

- **Dependency Management**: Like Maven, Gradle also has a powerful dependency management system. It's easy to add dependencies, and Gradle supports advanced dependency resolution strategies.

- **Build Caching and Incremental Builds**: Gradle's build cache and incremental build capabilities can lead to significantly faster build times, particularly in large, multi-module projects.

- **IDE Integration**: Gradle is well supported by all major IDEs (IntelliJ IDEA, Eclipse, etc.) and integrates seamlessly with Spring Boot projects.

Here is a Groovy example Gradle configuration for Spring Security 6:

```
dependencies {
    implementation 'org.springframework.boot:spring-boot-
    starter-security'
    implementation 'org.springframework.boot:spring-boot-
    starter-web'
}
```

Please consider these reasons when choosing between Maven and Gradle:

1. **Project Type**: If you're working on a simple, straightforward project or if your team is more familiar with Maven, it's often the better choice. Maven is stable and well supported, with a simpler, convention-driven setup.

2. **Project Complexity**: For more complex or multi-module projects, Gradle's flexibility and performance benefits make it a better choice. Gradle is also preferred in projects that require custom build logic or extensive automation.

3. **Team Preference and Familiarity**: Many organizations have established build practices. If your team has a preference or established standards (e.g., Maven), it's often more efficient to stick with that tool.

4. **Performance Needs**: Gradle generally performs faster than Maven, especially for large projects with many modules. If your project's build times are a priority, Gradle may be the better choice.

5. **Integration with Other Tools**: Both Maven and Gradle integrate well with CI/CD tools (like Jenkins, GitLab CI, and GitHub Actions), so choose the one that aligns best with your existing setup.

Shortly, you should use

- **Maven**: Best for projects needing convention, simplicity, and widespread team familiarity.

- **Gradle**: Ideal for complex projects needing flexibility, performance, and advanced customization.

For this book, I will use Maven 3.9.9.

Problem

How to install and configure Maven 3.9.9?

Solution

You can install Maven 3.9.9 by downloading the `.zip` file named `apache-maven-3.9.9-bin.zip` at this web page: `https://maven.apache.org/download.cgi`.

Unzip the file `apache-maven-3.9.9-bin.zip` as shown in Figure 1-6.

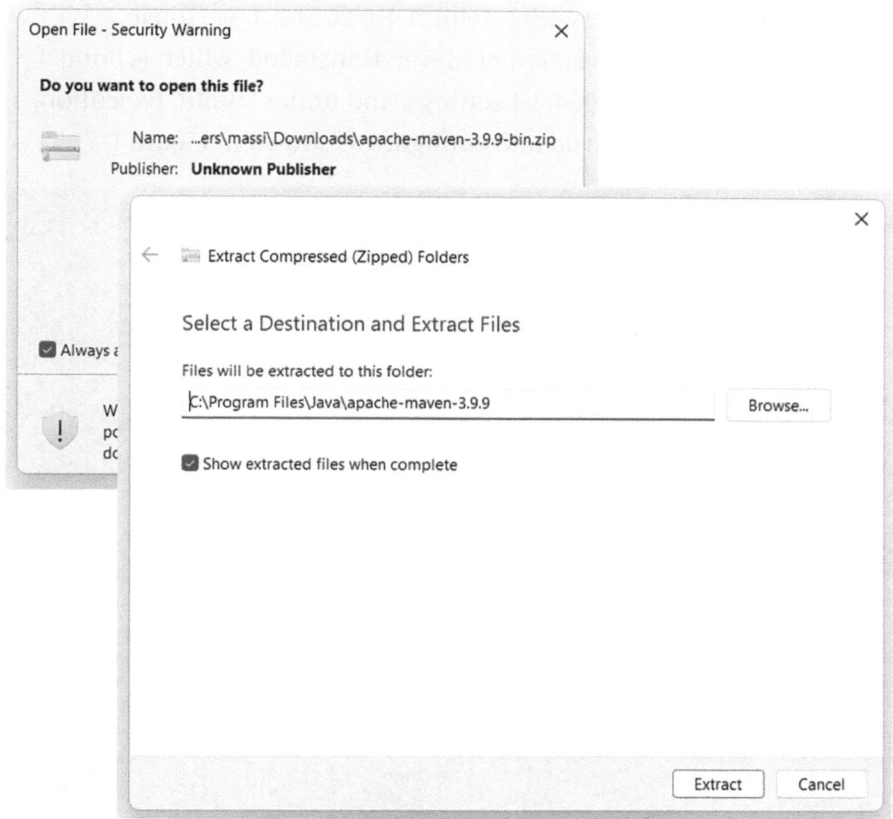

Figure 1-6. *Local Maven 3.9.9 installation*

Problem

How to install and configure the IntelliJ IDEA 2024.2.4 tool and configure Maven 3.9.9?

Solution

In order to use Maven 3.9.9 with IntelliJ IDEA 2024.2.4, we must configure where the local version of Maven is installed, which is done by opening IntelliJ IDEA 2024.2.4 settings, and under "Build, Execution, Development," choose Maven and configure as shown in Figure 1-7.

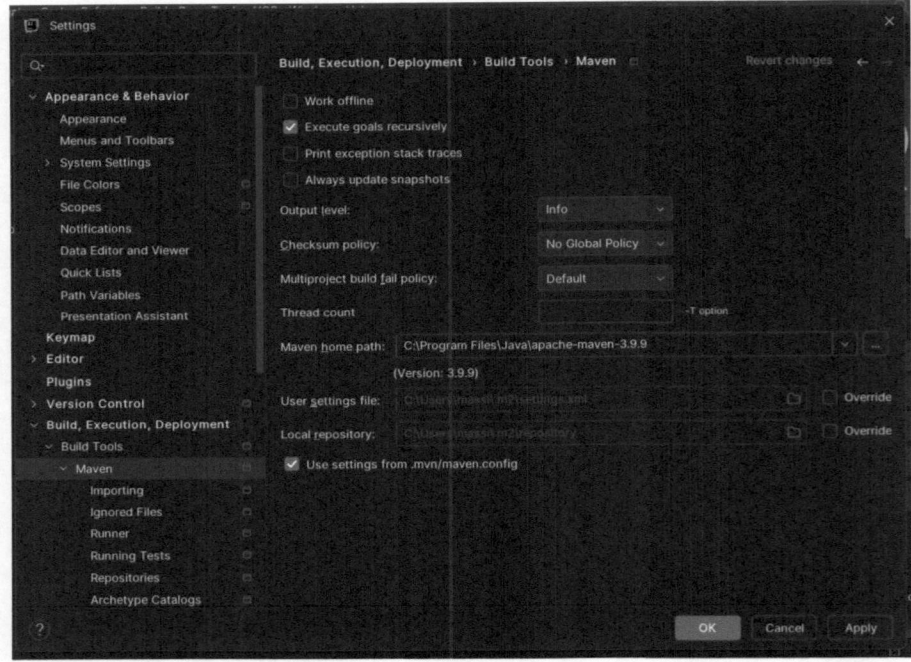

Figure 1-7. *Local Maven 3.9.9 is configured into IntelliJ IDEA 2024.2.4*

Now Maven 3.9.9 is ready to be used.

Problem

Why and when to use Apache Tomcat Server with Spring Security v6?

Solution

Using **Apache Tomcat** with **Spring Security 6** is a common choice for building secure, Java-based web applications due to a combination of Tomcat's stability, lightweight architecture, and compatibility with Spring Security's robust security features.

The combination of those provides a powerful, flexible, and secure environment for deploying Java-based web applications. Together, they offer

- Lightweight and efficient performance for secure applications

- Seamless integration, especially for projects built on the Spring ecosystem

- Advanced authentication, authorization, and session management features

- Flexible HTTPS and SSL/TLS configurations for secure communications

- Scalability and reliability, making Tomcat suitable for production deployments

Combining **Apache Tomcat** with **Spring Security 6** is ideal for organizations that need a stable and secure platform for web applications without the added complexity of a full Java EE application server. By leveraging Tomcat with Spring Security 6, you can build robust, secure applications that are both performant and easy to manage.

When using **Apache Tomcat** with **Spring Security 6**, you'll need to configure both the server and your Spring Security settings to ensure a secure, smooth deployment. Spring Security 6 is compatible with Apache Tomcat and brings powerful tools for managing authentication, authorization, and securing endpoints.

21

Problem

How to install and configure Apache Tomcat Server v11 to be used with Spring Security v6?

Solution

The first step is to download and install the Apache Tomcat Server v11 .exe file named apache-tomcat-11.0.0.exe at https://tomcat.apache.org/download-11.cgi.

Install the exe file to the default folder which is C:\Program Files\ Apache Software Foundation\Tomcat 11.0. Since you need to allow Spring projects to deploy to Tomcat Servers, you need to define Tomcat users to access to Tomcat Manager. This can be done when installing Tomcat v11 as shown in Figure 1-8 or manually by updating the file named tomcat-users.xml in the conf directory and adding the following XML fragment inside the <tomcat-users> element:

```
<role rolename="manager-gui"/>
<role rolename="manager-script"/>
<user username="tomcat" password="tomcat" roles="manager-gui,
manager-script"/>
```

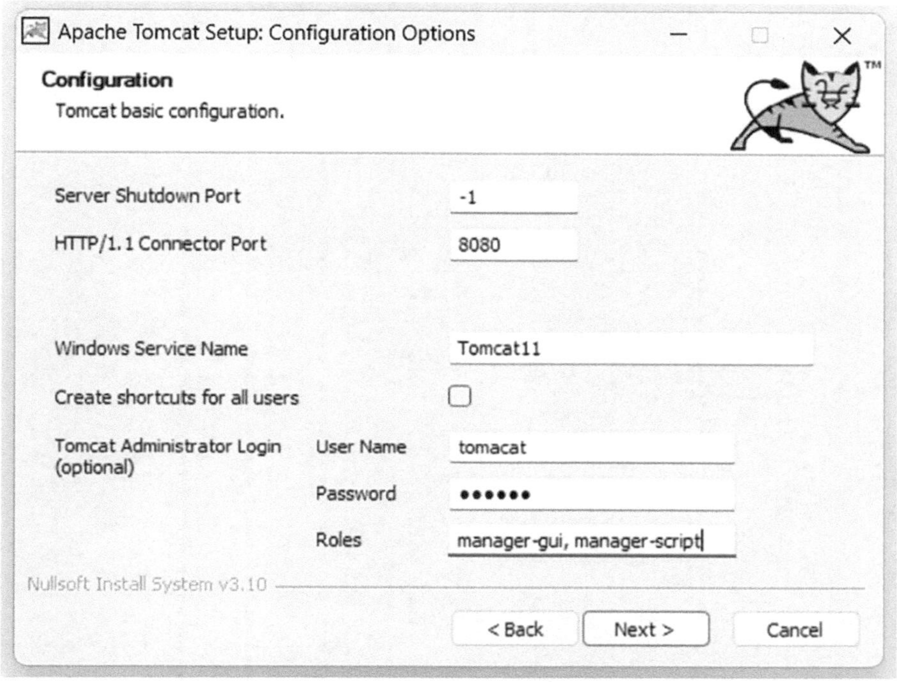

Figure 1-8. *Installation of Apache Tomcat v11 with new roles*

Now Apache Tomcat Server and plug-in v11 are ready to be used.

Problem

How to configure the right JDK package into the IntelliJ IDEA 2024.2.4 IDE tool?

Solution

Before starting a new Spring project, you want to make sure the right JDK package is installed into the IntelliJ IDEA 2024.2.4 IDE tool to compile your examples and avoid the typical compiling issue where the JRE is found instead of JDK. The configuration is shown in Figure 1-9.

23

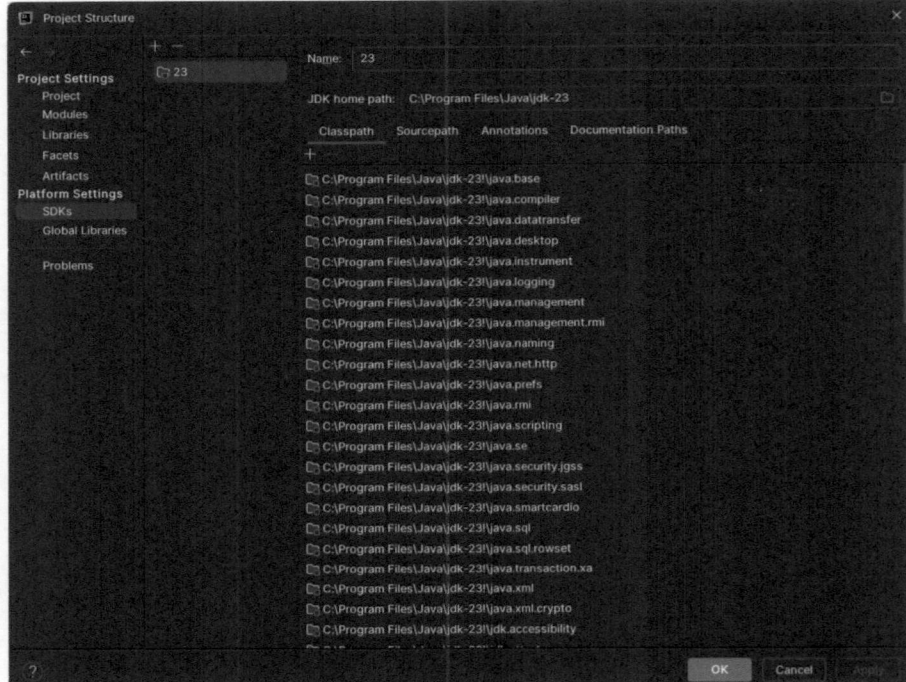

Figure 1-9. *Configuring the JDK to compile your examples*

So now the JDK compiler is set, and you are ready to start writing and running your first Spring web application example.

Summary

We introduced all the tools needed to create the environment to develop Spring Security Java Web Applications. You learned how to install and configure all the tools needed for these examples, and you should have a good idea of what is needed to build a Spring Security v6 project.

In the next chapter, you will learn how to build your first Java Web Application project.

CHAPTER 2

Java Web Application with Spring Security, JSP Tags, and Thymeleaf

After we set up all the needed development tools, we can now learn how to create a new Java Web Application project with Spring Security v6, JSP tags, and Thymeleaf.

Please note that for this example we will not use the Boot 3 Initializr tool to autogenerate our project, but instead we will learn how to write our own Java code.

With your development tools set up, you can now create your first Java Web Application project using IntelliJ IDEA 2024.2.4 with Spring Security v6, JSP tags, and Thymeleaf.

To create your first Java EE Web Application project in IntelliJ IDEA 2024.2.4, follow these steps:

1. Use the wizard to create a new Maven project.

2. Name the application Pss01, and add a .jsp file that displays "Hello Spring Security!"

3. Run the Web Application on Tomcat Server v11.

© Massimo Nardone 2025
M. Nardone, *Spring Security 6 Recipes*, Apress Pocket Guides,
https://doi.org/10.1007/979-8-8688-1297-2_2

This setup doesn't include security and is a basic introduction to building Java Web Applications with IntelliJ and Maven.

Problem

How do we create our first Web Application project?

Solution

As a first step, launch the IntelliJ IDEA tool and select File ➤ New ➤ Project ➤ Jakarta EE ➤ Web Application and fill out all information about the project, as shown in Figures 2-1 and 2-2.

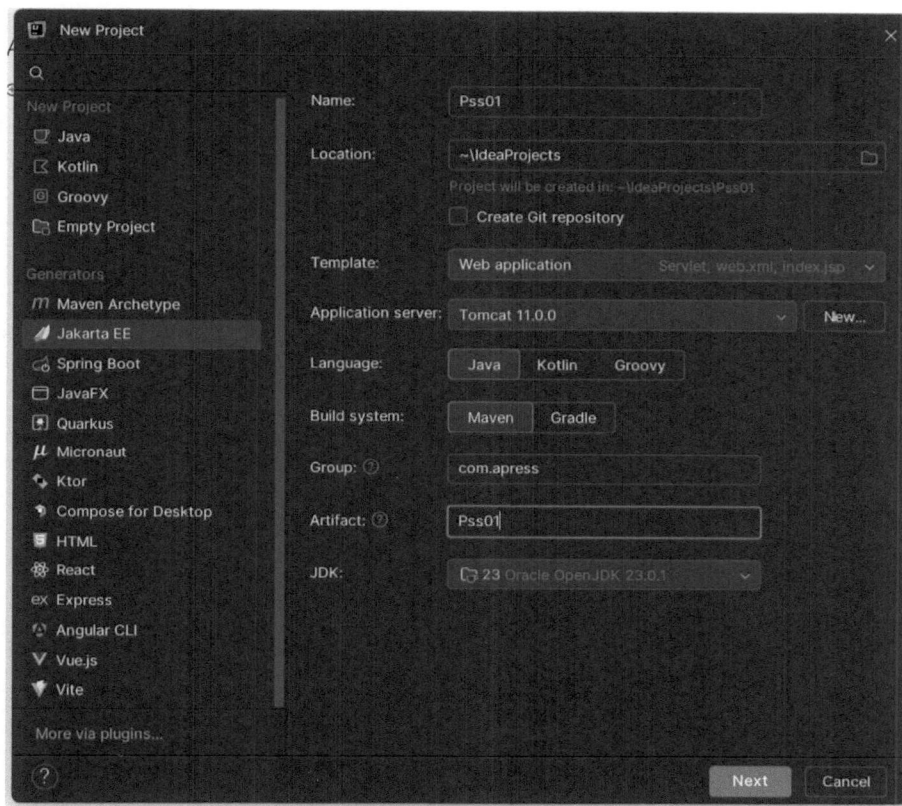

Figure 2-1. *Your first Java Web Application project*

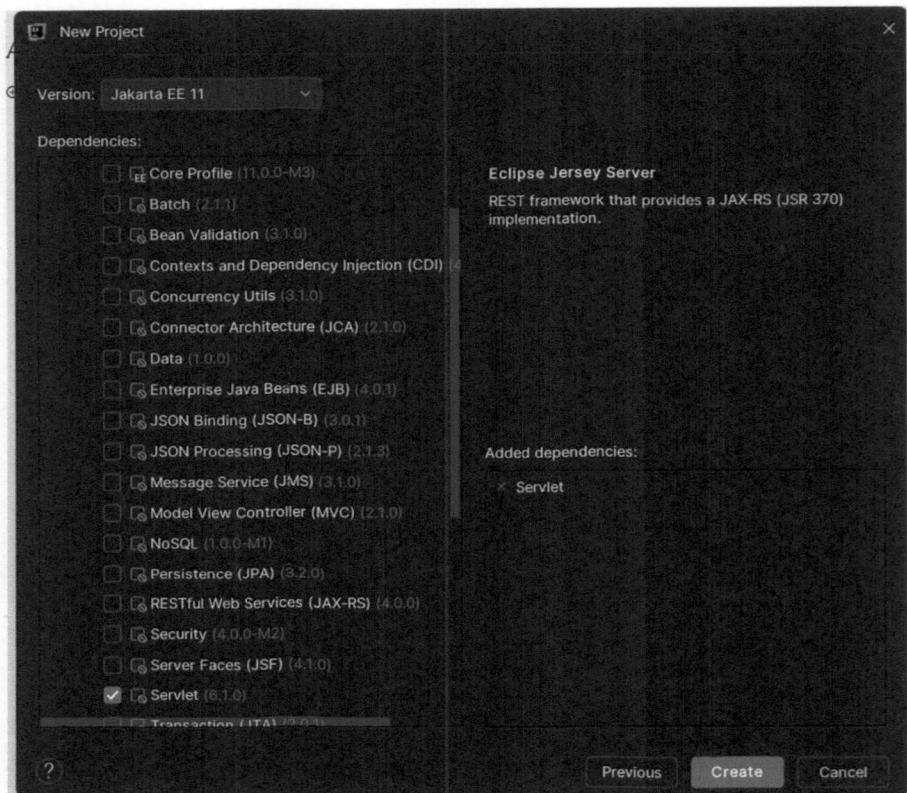

Figure 2-2. *Configuration for your first Java Web Application project*

In the Package Explorer, you should now see your Pss01 project. If you expand it and all its children, you'll see something like Figure 2-3.

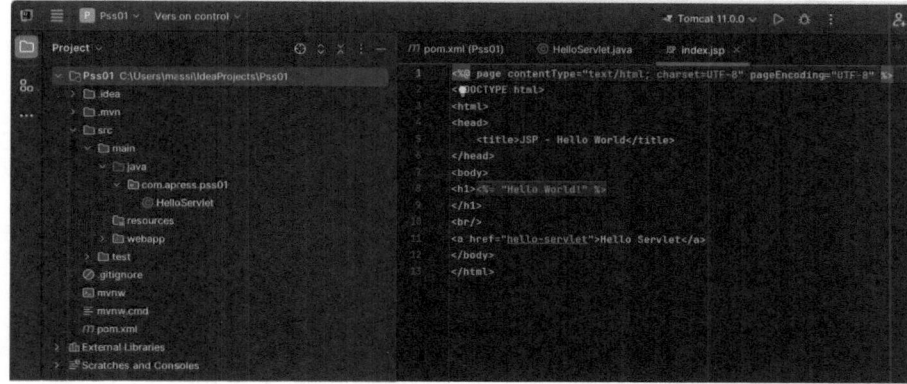

Figure 2-3. *Your first Java Web Application project structure*

In general, the structure of most Java Web Application projects will contain

- The target directory: Used to house all output of the build

- The src directory: Contains all of the source material for building the project, its site, etc.

- src/main/java: Application/library sources

- src/main/resources: Application/library resources

- web: Web application sources

- Pom.xml: File description of the project

Problem

How do we need to configure the pom.xml file?

Solution

Let's update the Java Web Application project's files needed for your first simple application. Please note that for this simple Java Web Application example, you will not need to add any specific dependency to the project file pom.xml, which looks initially like Listing 2-1.

Listing 2-1. The pom.xml file with servlet dependencies

```
<?xml version="1.0" encoding="UTF-8"?>
<project xmlns="http://maven.apache.org/POM/4.0.0"
         xmlns:xsi="http://www.w3.org/2001/XMLSchema-instance"
         xsi:schemaLocation="http://maven.apache.org/POM/4.0.0
https://maven.apache.org/xsd/maven-4.0.0.xsd">
  <modelVersion>4.0.0</modelVersion>

  <groupId>com.apress</groupId>
  <artifactId>Pss01</artifactId>
  <version>1.0-SNAPSHOT</version>
  <name>Pss01</name>
  <packaging>war</packaging>
```

The project right now only contains one simple .jsp file named index.jsp, which you will update to show the text you wish, as shown in Listing 2-2.

Listing 2-2. The index.jsp file

```
<%@ page contentType="text/html; charset=UTF-8"
pageEncoding="UTF-8" %>
<!DOCTYPE html>
<html>
```

```
<head>
    <title>My first Web Applications</title>
</head>
<body>
<h1><%= "Hello Spring Security v6!" %>
</h1>
</body>
</html>
```

Problem

How to configure and run our first Web Application?

Solution

Click the Add Configuration button, located at the top right of the IntelliJ tool, to configure how to run your first example.

You can run your project using the external Tomcat Server v10, as shown in Figure 2-4.

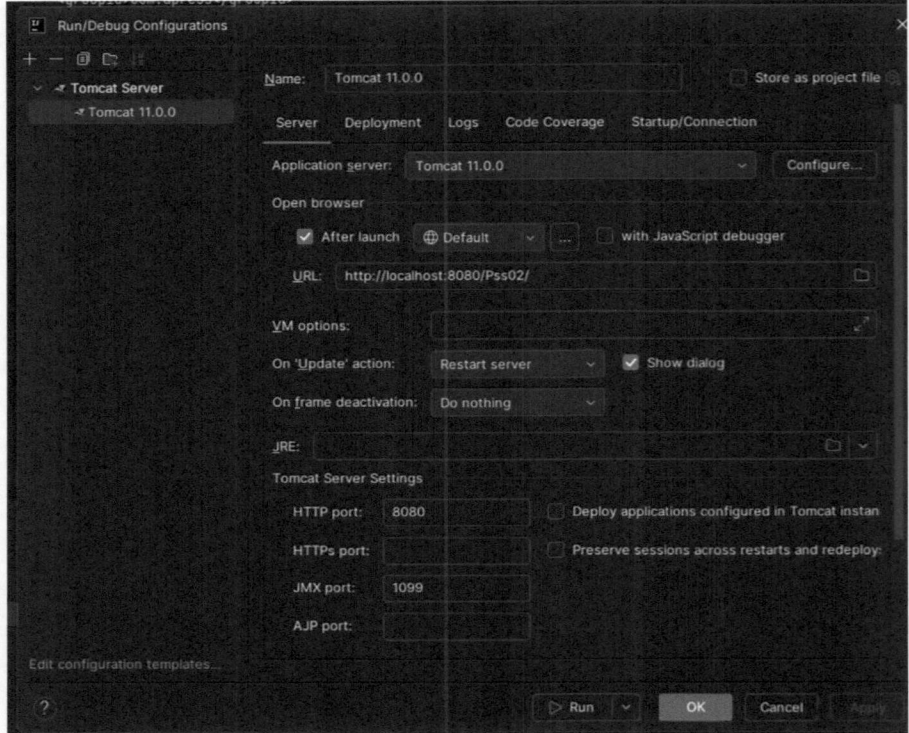

Figure 2-4. *Configure the running steps of your first Maven project*

Now you can open your web browser and type the web address
`http://localhost:8080/Pss01`, as shown in Figure 2-5.

Figure 2-5. *The Java Web Application project running in a
web browser*

Your first Java Web Application project was done now, so let's create a new Spring Security 6 project.

Spring Security integrates well with the Spring ecosystem, allowing developers to start simple and learn advanced concepts over time.

There are two ways to create a new Spring project.

You can either create a Spring project via Spring Initializr, which we will learn in Chapter 3, or via any IDE tool, which in this case is IntelliJ IDEA 2024.2.4.

To build a basic Spring Security example, you could set up a Maven project where users need to authenticate as "user" or "admin" to access secure resources.

If you use the stand-alone installation of the Spring Security reference release and choose not to use an IDE to build your Maven project, you'll notice multiple folders in the installation directory. Each folder typically represents a subproject or module, dividing Spring Security's functionality into distinct and specialized components.

Problem

Where can I find and what includes the Spring Security v6 source package?

Solution

Open source software has an invaluable characteristic for software developers: free access to all source code. With this, we can understand how our favorite tools and frameworks work internally, and we also can learn a lot about the way other (perhaps very good) developers work, including what practices, techniques, and patterns they use. Free access to source code also enables us, in general, to gather ideas and experience for our own development. As a more practical matter, having access to the source code allows us to debug these applications in the context of our application; we can find bugs or simply follow our application's execution through them.

Currently, Spring Security and most Spring projects live in GitHub. You probably know about GitHub (`https://github.com/`). If you don't, you should definitely take a look at it because it has become a standard public source code repository for many open source projects in a multitude of programming languages.

GitHub is a repository and a hosting service for Git repositories, with a very friendly management interface. The Spring Security project can be found inside the SpringSource general GitHub section at `https://github.com/spring-projects/spring-security`.

To get the code, just download and install it.

A short description of some of the most important modules included in Spring Security v6 can be found at `https://docs.spring.io/spring-security/reference/modules.html`

The most important modules include

- Core: spring-security-core.jar

- Remoting: spring-security-remoting.jar

- Web: spring-security-web.jar

- Config: spring-security-config.jar

- LDAP: spring-security-ldap.jar

- OAuth 2.0 Core: spring-security-oauth2-core.jar

- OAuth 2.0 Client: spring-security-oauth2-client.jar

- OAuth 2.0 JOSE: spring-security-oauth2-jose.jar

- OAuth 2.0 Resource Server: spring-security-oauth2-resource-server.jar

- ACL: spring-security-acl.jar

- CAS: spring-security-cas.jar

- Test: spring-security-test.jar

- Taglibs: spring-security-taglibs.jar

Problem

How do we add Spring Security v6 to our previous Maven Java Web Application?

Solution

Let's create a new one named "Pss02" and add Spring Security v6 in it.

Here are the steps you will follow to build the simple Spring Security Maven Web Application project:

- Import the required Spring Framework and Spring Security v6 libraries into the project (into the pom. xml file).

- Configure the project to be aware of Spring Security.

- Configure the users and roles that will be part of the system.

- Configure the URLs that you want to secure.

- Create all needed Java and web files.

- Run the Spring Security v6 project using the external Tomcat Server v11.

Since we are using Maven, the first step will be including Spring Security jar dependencies in pom.xml, which are

- spring-security-core

- spring-security-config

- spring-security-web

- spring-webmvc

Here are the Maven dependencies you must add to the pom.xml file:

```
<dependency>
      <groupId>org.springframework.security</groupId>
      <artifactId>spring-security-core</artifactId>
      <version>6.3.2</version>
  </dependency>
  <dependency>
      <groupId>org.springframework.security</groupId>
      <artifactId>spring-security-config</artifactId>
      <version>6.1.4</version>
  </dependency>
  <dependency>
      <groupId>org.springframework.security</groupId>
      <artifactId>spring-security-web</artifactId>
      <version>6.1.0</version>
  </dependency>
  <dependency>
      <groupId>org.springframework</groupId>
      <artifactId>spring-webmvc</artifactId>
      <version>6.1.13</version>
  </dependency>
```

We will then update the index.jsp page as shown in Listing 2-3.

Listing 2-3. index.jsp

```
<%@ page contentType="text/html; charset=UTF-8"
pageEncoding="UTF-8" %>
<!DOCTYPE html>
<html>
<head>
    <title>Welcome to Spring Security 6 authentication
    example!</title>
</head>
<body>
<h2>Welcome to Spring Security 6 authentication example!</h2>

<h2>You are an authenticated user!</h2>

</body>
</html>
```

Since we added Spring Security to the project, it will secure the entire project by default, given a generated security password to be entered together with "user" as the username. So when we type localhost:8080, Spring will require us to provide the newly created username "user" and password "e6fd5a38-b7a8-4d55-b47a-9ece6e3341fa" to log in, as shown in Figure 2-6.

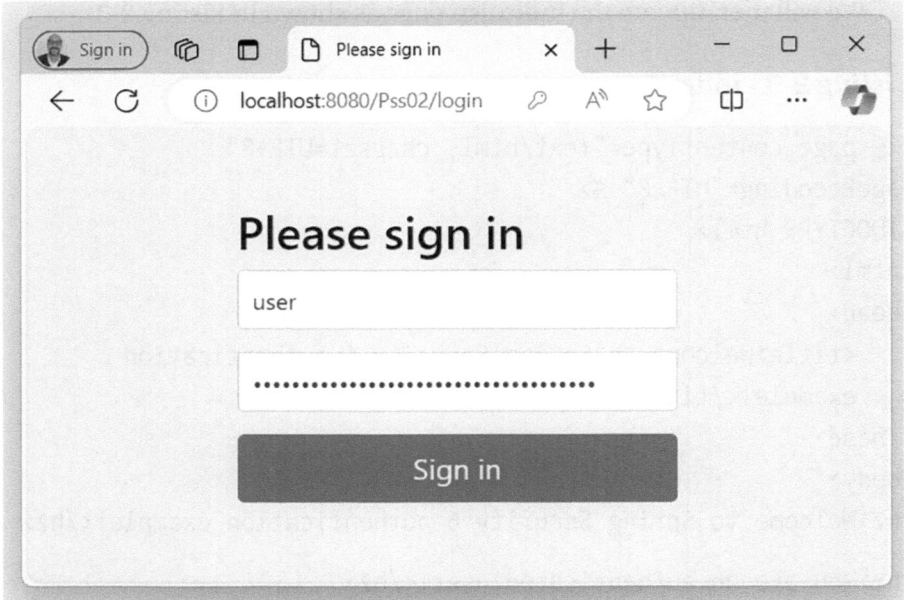

Figure 2-6. *Secure Spring application with login page*

If we enter the wrong password, we will get the message shown in Figure 2-7.

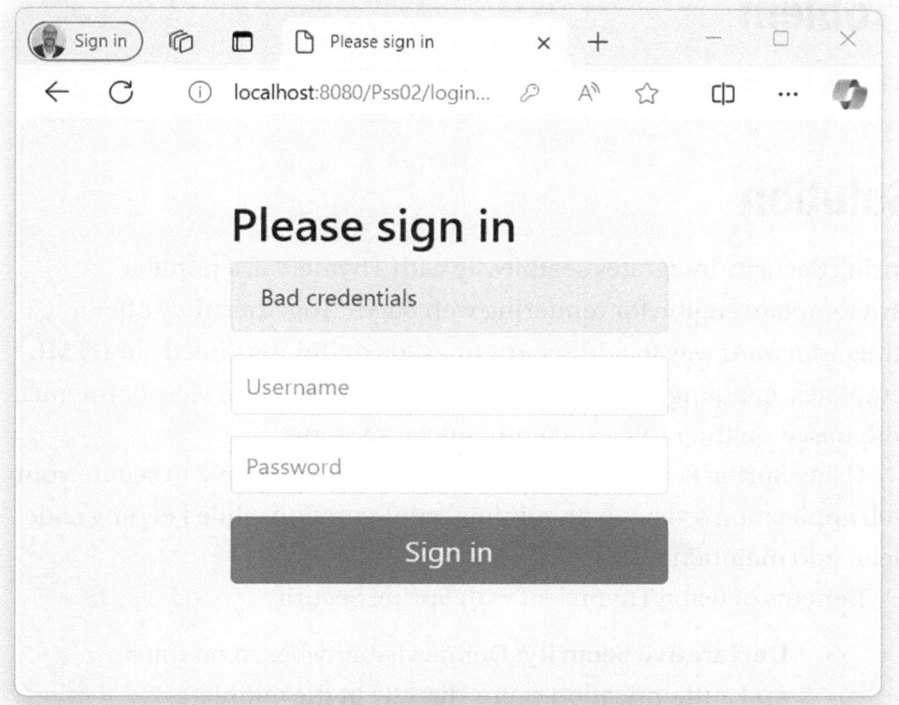

Figure 2-7. *Unsuccessful login message*

If we enter the right username and password, we will get the "Welcome to Spring Security 6" message as shown in Figure 2-8.

Figure 2-8. *Successful login message*

Problem

What is Thymeleaf and when to use it?

Solution

Spring Security integrates seamlessly with Thymeleaf, a popular Java template engine for rendering web pages. Together, they offer a straightforward way to add security-based conditions directly in HTML templates, enabling control over what content users can view or interact with based on their roles and authentication status.

Using Spring Security with Thymeleaf makes it simple to secure your web application's views with minimal configuration while keeping code clean and maintainable.

Benefits of using Thymeleaf with Spring Security

- **Declarative Security**: Define visibility based on roles and authentication status directly in the template.

- **Readability**: Keeps security logic clear and within the view layer.

- **Seamless Integration**: Using thymeleaf-extras-springsecurity6, you can handle secure URLs, user information, and content visibility without extra backend code.

Thymeleaf security expressions include

- isAuthenticated(): Checks if a user is logged in

- isAnonymous(): Checks if a user is not logged in

- hasRole('ROLE_NAME'): Checks if a user has a specific role

- hasAuthority('authority'): Equivalent to hasRole but more generic, allowing granular authorities

- principal: Accesses the authenticated user's details (e.g., principal.username)

Spring Security provides an extra library for Thymeleaf integration, called thymeleaf-extras-springsecurity6, if you are using Spring Security v6, or check the version that matches your Spring Security.

Problem

How to add Thymeleaf dependency to your pom.xml if you're using Maven?

Solution

```
<dependency>
    <groupId>org.thymeleaf.extras</groupId>
    <artifactId>thymeleaf-extras-springsecurity6</artifactId>
    <version>3.1.1.RELEASE</version>
</dependency>
```

Problem

How to add Thymeleaf and Spring Security attributes?

Solution

Here are some of the most useful attributes for managing security in Thymeleaf templates:

41

- sec:authorize="expression": Controls visibility based
  on an expression. Content is rendered only if the
  expression evaluates to true.

```
<!-- Only visible to authenticated users -->
<div sec:authorize="isAuthenticated()">
    Welcome, <span sec:authentication=
    "name">User</span>!
</div>
```

```
<!-- Only visible to users with ROLE_ADMIN -->
<div sec:authorize="hasRole('ROLE_ADMIN')">
    Admin Section
</div>
sec:authentication="property": Displays information
about the authenticated user.
```

```
<!-- Display the current user's username -->
<span sec:authentication="name">Username</span>
sec:authorize="isAnonymous()": Renders content only if
the user is not logged in (anonymous).
```

```
<!-- Show login link to unauthenticated users -->
<a sec:authorize="isAnonymous()" href="/
login">Login</a>
```

Problem

What are JSP tags and when to use them?

Solution

Spring Security provides a set of JSP tags to make it easier to manage and control security within JSP pages. These tags allow you to show or hide content based on the user's authentication status, roles, and other security-related conditions.

Using these tags in JSP makes it easy to handle user permissions and roles directly in the view layer without extensive Java code, helping keep your application secure and maintainable.

Problem

What are the most commonly used Spring Security JSP tags?

Solution

- Authentication Tags

  ```
  <sec:authentication>: Displays information about the
  current authentication.
  <sec:authentication property="name" /> <!-- Displays
  the username -->
  ```

- Access Control Tags

  ```
  <sec:authorize access="expression">...</sec:authorize>:
  Restricts access to parts of a JSP page based on
  security expressions.
  <sec:authorize access="hasRole('ADMIN')">
    <!-- Only users with the 'ADMIN' role can see this
    content -->
    <p>Welcome, Admin!</p>
  ```

```
</sec:authorize>
<sec:authorize ifAllGranted="roles"
ifAnyGranted="roles" ifNotGranted="roles">...
</sec:authorize>: Controls content visibility based
on roles.
<sec:authorize ifAllGranted="ROLE_USER, ROLE_ADMIN">
  <!-- Content for users with both USER and ADMIN
  roles -->
</sec:authorize>
<sec:authorize ifAnyGranted="ROLE_USER, ROLE_GUEST">
  <!-- Content for users with either USER or GUEST
  roles -->
</sec:authorize>
<sec:authorize ifNotGranted="ROLE_ADMIN">
  <!-- Content for users who do NOT have the ADMIN
  role -->
</sec:authorize>
```

- Logout Tag

```
<sec:logout />: Generates a link to log out the
current user.
<a href="<sec:logout />">Logout</a>
```

- URL Tag

```
<sec:url value="path" />: Generates a secure URL
(useful for adding CSRF tokens to URLs in forms).
<form action="<sec:url value='/processForm' />"
method="post">
  <!-- form content here -->
</form>
```

We will add the following lines to our code to adopt the JSP tags:

```
<dependency>
    <groupId>org.springframework.security</groupId>
    <artifactId>spring-security-taglibs</artifactId>
    <version>6.1.5</version>
</dependency>
```

The updated project file pom.xml with Spring Security 6 and all tools described is shown in Listing 2-4.

Listing 2-4. pom.xml file

```
<?xml version="1.0" encoding="UTF-8"?>
<project xmlns="http://maven.apache.org/POM/4.0.0"
         xmlns:xsi="http://www.w3.org/2001/XMLSchema-instance"
         xsi:schemaLocation="http://maven.apache.org/POM/4.0.0
         https://maven.apache.org/xsd/maven-4.0.0.xsd">
    <modelVersion>4.0.0</modelVersion>

    <groupId>com.apress</groupId>
    <artifactId>Pss02</artifactId>
    <version>1.0-SNAPSHOT</version>
    <name>Pss02</name>
    <packaging>war</packaging>

    <properties>
        <project.build.sourceEncoding>UTF-8</project.build.
        sourceEncoding>
        <maven.compiler.target>11</maven.compiler.target>
        <maven.compiler.source>11</maven.compiler.source>
        <junit.version>5.9.2</junit.version>
    </properties>
```

```
<dependencies>
   <dependency>
        <groupId>org.springframework.security</groupId>
        <artifactId>spring-security-core</artifactId>
        <version>6.3.2</version>
   </dependency>
   <dependency>
        <groupId>org.springframework.security</groupId>
        <artifactId>spring-security-config</artifactId>
        <version>6.1.4</version>
   </dependency>
   <dependency>
        <groupId>org.springframework.security</groupId>
        <artifactId>spring-security-web</artifactId>
        <version>6.1.0</version>
   </dependency>
   <dependency>
        <groupId>org.springframework.security</groupId>
        <artifactId>spring-security-taglibs</artifactId>
        <version>6.1.5</version>
   </dependency>

   <dependency>
        <groupId>org.springframework</groupId>
        <artifactId>spring-webmvc</artifactId>
        <version>6.1.13</version>
   </dependency>
   <dependency>
        <groupId>jakarta.servlet</groupId>
        <artifactId>jakarta.servlet-api</artifactId>
        <version>5.0.0</version>
```

```
            <scope>provided</scope>
        </dependency>
        <dependency>
            <groupId>org.junit.jupiter</groupId>
            <artifactId>junit-jupiter-api</artifactId>
            <version>${junit.version}</version>
            <scope>test</scope>
        </dependency>
        <dependency>
            <groupId>org.junit.jupiter</groupId>
            <artifactId>junit-jupiter-engine</artifactId>
            <version>${junit.version}</version>
            <scope>test</scope>
        </dependency>
    </dependencies>

    <build>
        <plugins>
            <plugin>
                <groupId>org.apache.maven.plugins</groupId>
                <artifactId>maven-war-plugin</artifactId>
                <version>3.3.2</version>
            </plugin>
        </plugins>
    </build>
</project>
```

Problem

How to configure and customize Spring Security v6 to our project?

Solution

To activate Spring Security Web project configuration in your Maven
Web Application, you need to configure a particular servlet filter that will
take care of preprocessing and postprocessing the requests, as well as
managing the required security constraints.

We will start creating a Java package where all your Java classes will be
located:

- com.apress.pss02.springsecurity.configuration

Then you need to define the Java classes needed for your example
under package configuration:

- SecurityConfiguration

- AppInitializer

- SpringSecurityInitializer

In this example, we will learn how to enable Spring Security v6
using the annotation named "@EnableWebSecurity" without using the
WebSecurityConfigurerAdapter class, but instead building this example on
top of the spring webmvc hibernate integration example.

We will create a new Java Spring Security configuration class named
"SecurityConfiguration" which will utilize "@EnableWebSecurity"
annotation, to help us to configure the Spring Security–related beans such
as WebSecurityConfigurer and SecurityFilterChain.

Problem

How do we add security configuration to a Java Web Application?

Solution

In this new Spring Security v6 "SecurityConfiguration" Java class, shown in Listing 2-5, we will need to

1. Create two demo in-memory users named "user" and "admin" which will be authorized to access a secure resource of the project.

2. Use BCryptPasswordEncoder to encode the user passwords for added security.

3. Configure the SecurityFilterChain bean with the HTTP-based method login to the application as basic-auth.

Listing 2-5. SecurityConfiguration Java class

```
package com.apress.pss02.configuration;

import org.springframework.context.annotation.Bean;
import org.springframework.context.annotation.Configuration;
import org.springframework.security.config.annotation.web.
builders.HttpSecurity;
import org.springframework.security.config.annotation.web.
configuration.EnableWebSecurity;
import org.springframework.security.core.userdetails.User;
import org.springframework.security.core.userdetails.
UserDetails;
import org.springframework.security.core.userdetails.
UserDetailsService;
import org.springframework.security.crypto.bcrypt.
BCryptPasswordEncoder;
import org.springframework.security.crypto.password.
PasswordEncoder;
```

```java
import org.springframework.security.provisioning.
InMemoryUserDetailsManager;
import org.springframework.security.web.SecurityFilterChain;

import static org.springframework.security.config.
Customizer.withDefaults;

@Configuration
@EnableWebSecurity

public class SecurityConfiguration {

    @Bean
    public SecurityFilterChain filterChain1(HttpSecurity http)
    throws Exception {
        http
                .authorizeHttpRequests((authorize) -> authorize
                        .anyRequest().authenticated()

                )
                .formLogin(withDefaults());
        return http.build();
    }

    @Bean
    public UserDetailsService userDetailsService(){

        UserDetails user = User.builder()
                .username("user")
                .password(passwordEncoder().
                encode("userpassw"))
                .roles("USER")
                .build();

        UserDetails admin = User.builder()
                .username("admin")
```

```
                    .password(passwordEncoder().encode("adminpassw"))
                    .roles("ADMIN")
                    .build();

        return new InMemoryUserDetailsManager(user, admin);
    }

    @Bean
    public static PasswordEncoder passwordEncoder(){
        return new BCryptPasswordEncoder();
    }

}
```

Problem

How do we initialize Spring Security to our Java classes?

Solution

As Spring Security is implemented using DelegatingFilterProxy, our next step will be to create a new Java class named "SpringSecurityInitializer" used for initializing Spring Security using the AbstractSecurityWebApplicationInitializer class so that Spring will

- Detect the instance of this class during application startup

- Register the DelegatingFilterProxy to use the springSecurityFilterChain before any other registered filter

- Register a ContextLoaderListener

The "SpringSecurityInitializer" Java class is shown in Listing 2-6.

Listing 2-6. SpringSecurityInitializer Java class

```
package com.apress.pss02.configuration;

import org.springframework.security.web.context.AbstractSecurity
WebApplicationInitializer;

public class SpringSecurityInitializer extends AbstractSecurity
WebApplicationInitializer {

    //no code needed
}
```

We will next need to include our SecurityConfiguration.class to the new "AppInitializer" Java class, used to initialize the HibernateConfig, SecurityConfiguration, and WebMvcConfig classes, as shown in Listing 2-7.

Listing 2-7. AppInitializer Java class

```
package com.apress.pss02.configuration;

import jakarta.servlet.ServletContext;
import org.springframework.security.access.SecurityConfig;

import org.springframework.web.WebApplicationInitializer;
import org.springframework.web.context.ContextLoaderListener;
import org.springframework.web.context.support.
AnnotationConfigWebApplicationContext;
import org.springframework.web.filter.DelegatingFilterProxy;

public class AppInitializer implements
WebApplicationInitializer {

    @Override
    public void onStartup(ServletContext sc) {
```

```
AnnotationConfigWebApplicationContext root = new Annota
tionConfigWebApplicationContext();
root.register(SecurityConfiguration.class);

sc.addListener(new ContextLoaderListener(root));

sc.addFilter("securityFilter", new DelegatingFilter
Proxy("springSecurityFilterChain"))
        .addMappingForUrlPatterns(null, false, "/*");
    }
}
```

Finally, we will update the index.jsp page as shown in Listing 2-8.

Listing 2-8. index.jsp

```
<%@ taglib prefix="sec" uri="http://www.springframework.crg/
security/tags" %>
<%@ page contentType="text/html; charset=UTF-8"
pageEncoding="UTF-8" %>

<!DOCTYPE html>
<html>
<head>
    <title>Welcome to Spring Security 6 authentication
    example!</title>
</head>
<body>
<h2>Welcome to Spring Security 6 authentication example!</h2>

<sec:authorize access="isAuthenticated()">
    <h2>You are an authenticated user: <sec:authentication
    property="name"/></h2>
</sec:authorize>

</body>
</html>
```

The index.jsp page, using the JSP tags configured, will display the username of the authenticated user.

The structure of your new Spring Security v6 project should look like Figure 2-9.

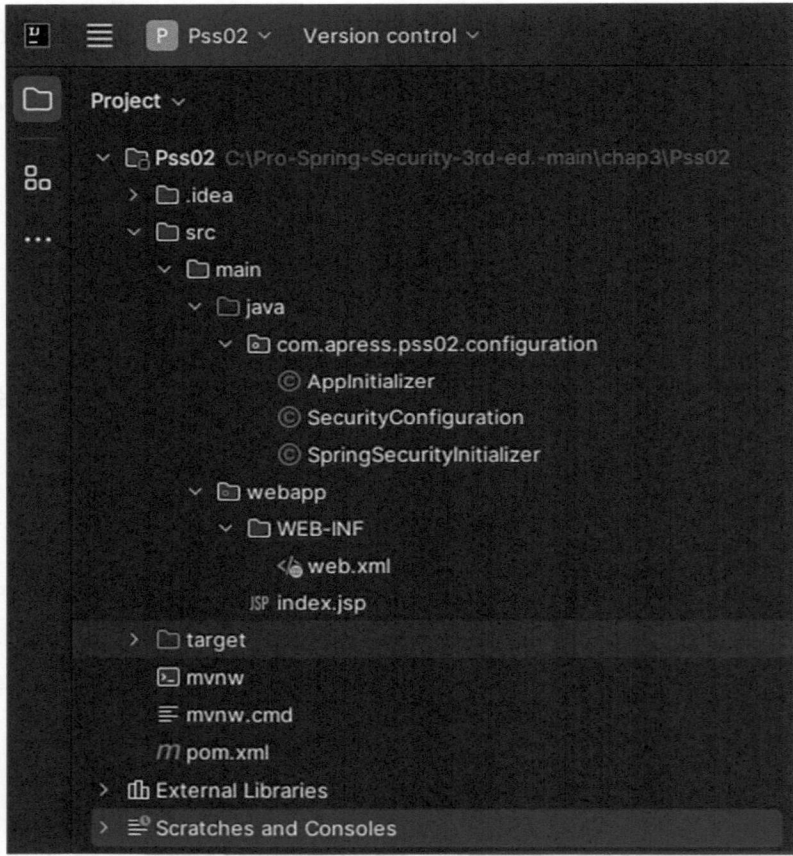

Figure 2-9. *New Spring Security v6 project structure*

Next, build and run the Spring Security v6 project using Tomcat v11 as shown in Figure 2-10.

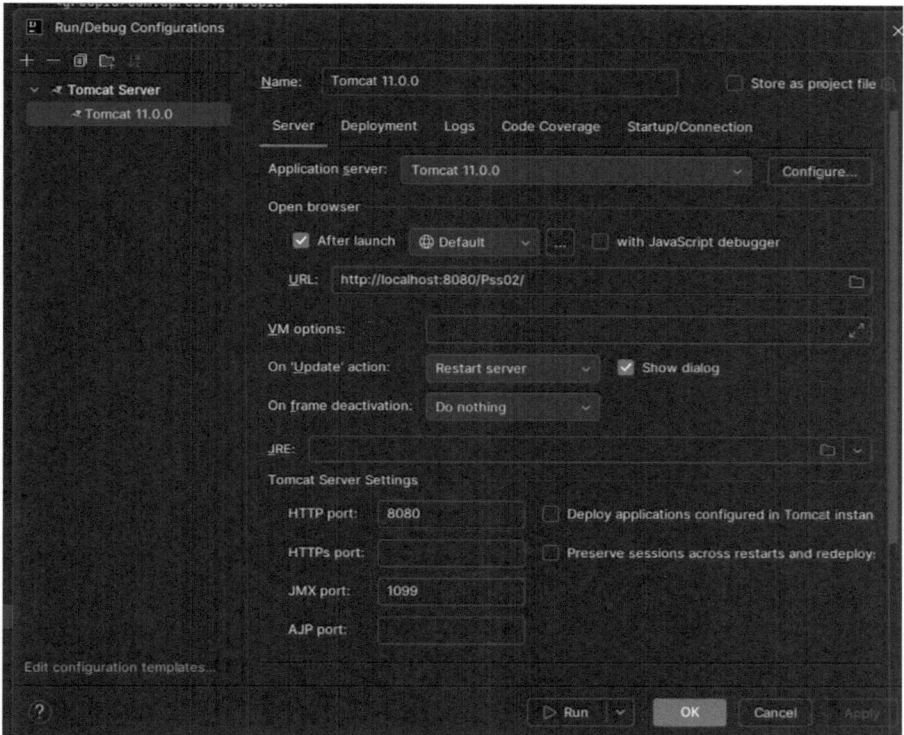

Figure 2-10. *Project running configuration using Tomcat v11*

You can now build the project, deploy the JAR file, start the application running on the stand-alone Tomcat Server v11, and deploy the JAR file automatically.

Your application is deployed successfully; the web browser will open automatically the following link: `http://localhost:8080/Pss02/login/`.

Now, if you access with the wrong credentials, you will receive an error message like the one in Figure 2-11.

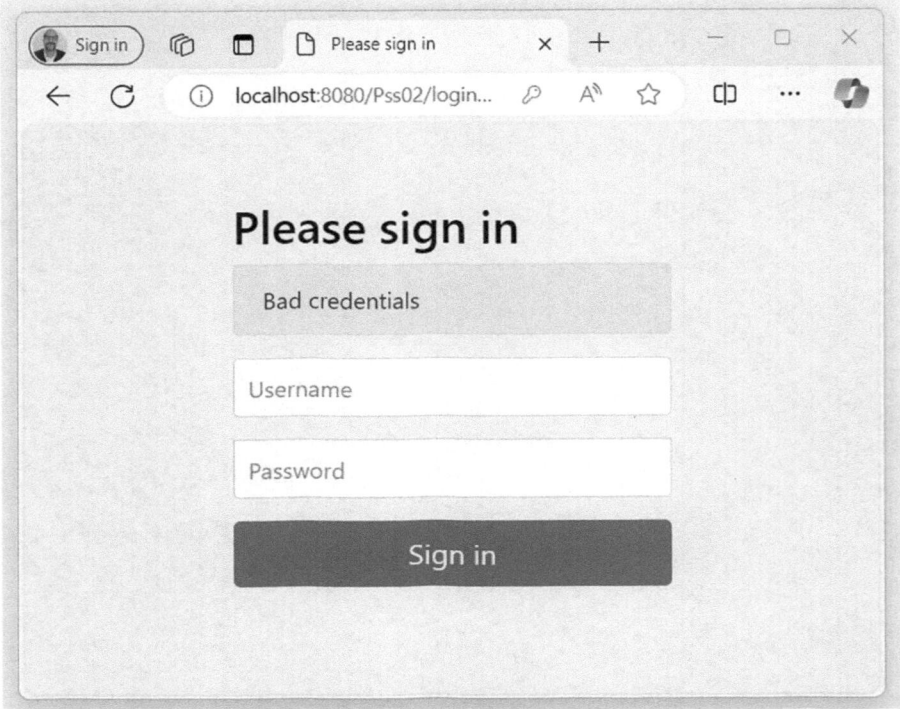

Figure 2-11. *Accessing with wrong login credentials*

As you can see, Spring Security will directly produce the login error and remind the user that the credentials provided are not correct.

If you next provide the right user or admin credentials, you will receive the content defined in the index.jsp page, which identifies if an admin or user credential is provided and displays a welcome message with the username authenticated.

In our case, we will, for example, authenticate using the admin credential as shown in Figure 2-12.

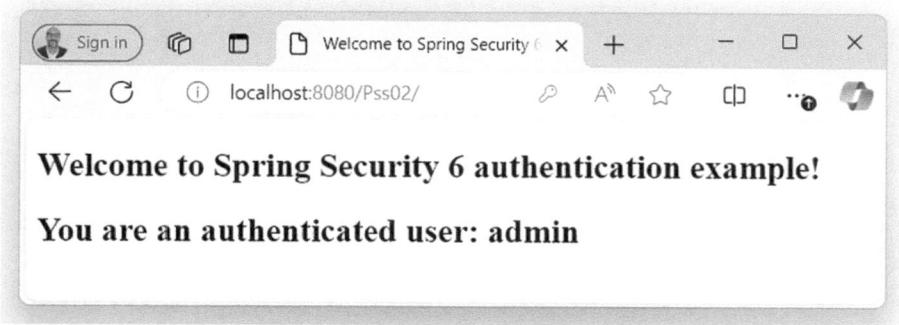

Figure 2-12. *Welcome page for admin authenticated user*

Great! You have built your first Spring Security v6 web application. We will dive deeply into how all this works internally when we look at the architecture of Spring Security.

Summary

We introduced all the tools needed to create the environment to develop Spring Security Java Web Applications, such as JSP tags and Thymeleaf.

You learned how to install and configure all the tools needed for these examples, and you should have a good idea of what is needed to build a Spring Security v6 project. You learned how to build your first Java Web Application project without Spring Security, and then you added the security dependencies to update it as a Spring Security v6 application.

In the next chapter, we will learn how to develop a Spring Security Java Web Application using Spring Boot 3 Initializr.

CHAPTER 3

Java Web Application and Spring Boot 3 Initializr

In this chapter, we will learn how to build a Java Web Application using Spring Security 6 in Spring Boot 3. You will see in detail the inner work of the security filter chain and the different metadata options at your disposal to define security constraints in your application.

You will also learn how to build a custom login form.

Let's build your Java Web Application using Spring Security 6 in Spring Boot 3, and please make sure you're using Java 17+, as the baseline for Spring Boot 3 and Spring Security 6 is now Java 17. We will use Java v23 in this demo.

Let's build our project with the Spring Boot 3 Initializr.

As a first step, you will create a new Spring project named pss01_Security using the Spring Initializr web tool at `https://start.spring.io/` as shown in Figure 3-1.

For our example, we chose Java 23, Maven, and JAR, with Spring Security and Web as dependencies.

© Massimo Nardone 2025
M. Nardone, *Spring Security 6 Recipes*, Apress Pocket Guides,
https://doi.org/10.1007/979-8-8688-1297-2_3

Figure 3-1. *New Spring project using Spring Initializr*

Once the project is generated, unzip the file and open the project with your IDE tool in use.

Our new project files and the pss01_Security project structure are shown in Figure 3-2.

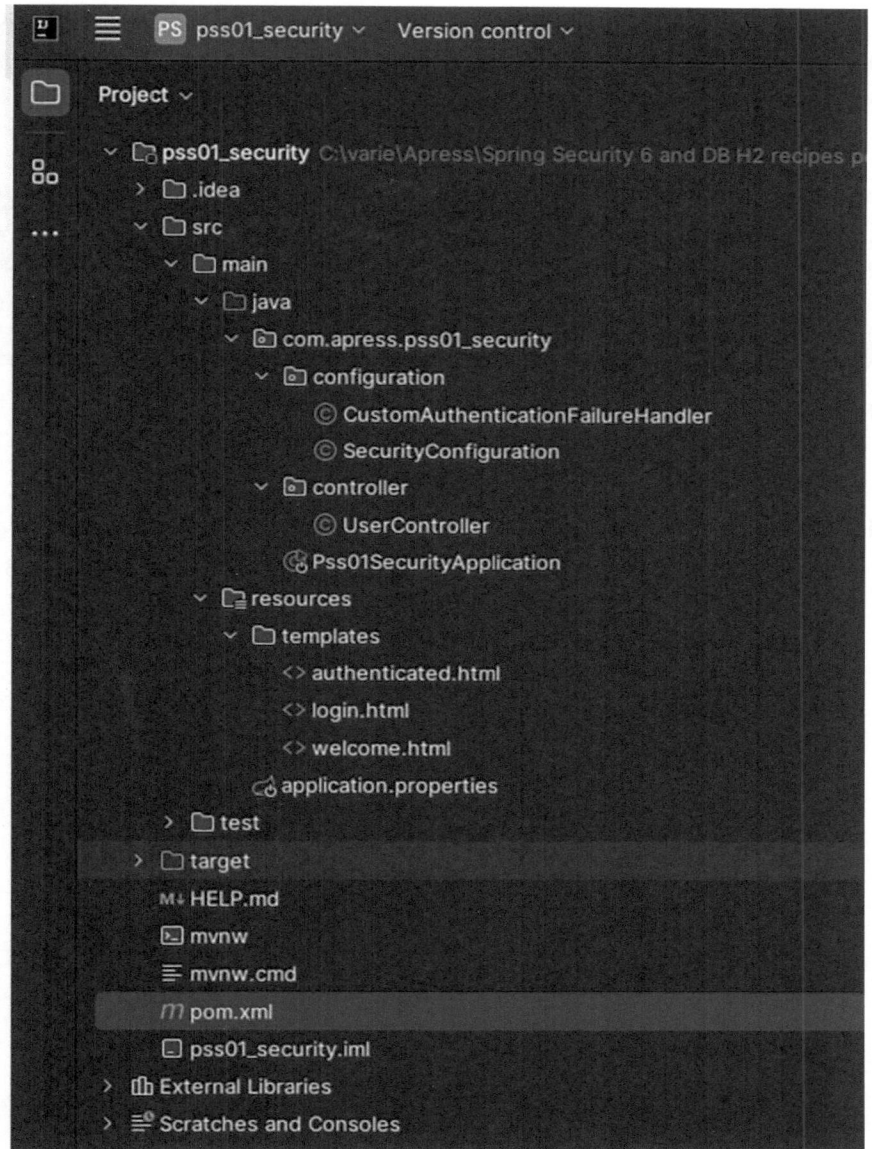

Figure 3-2. *New Spring project structure*

If, like in our example, Spring Security is on the classpath, Spring Boot automatically secures all HTTP endpoints with "basic" authentication, generating a security password to be used as a credential with the "user" as the username, as shown in Figure 3-3.

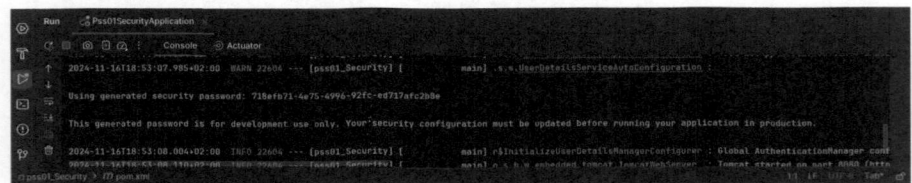

Figure 3-3. *Running the new Spring project*

This means that now if we go ahead and type localhost:8080, Spring will require us to provide the newly created username "user" and password "718efb71-4e73-4996-92fc-ed717afc2b8e" to log in, as shown in Figure 3-4.

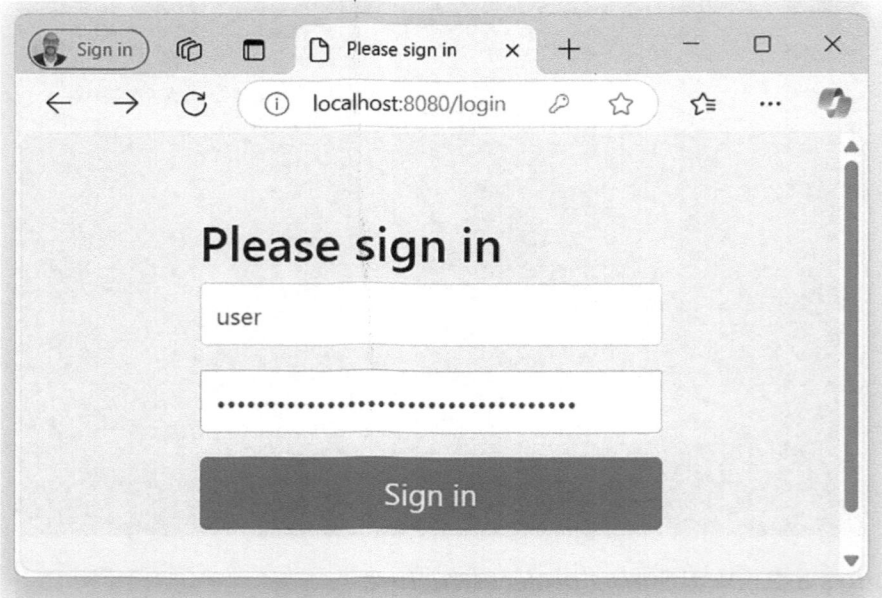

Figure 3-4. *Secure Spring application with login page*

Since our web application is based on Spring MVC, we need to configure Spring MVC and set up view controllers to expose the HTML templates we will create later.

Problem

How do we create a Controller Java class?

Solution

Let's create a simple controller to get a simple "Welcome to Spring Security 6" message when entering the right login information, as shown in Listing 3-1.

Listing 3-1. A simple UserController Java class

```java
package com.apress.pss01_Security;

import org.springframework.web.bind.annotation.GetMapping;
import org.springframework.web.bind.annotation.RestController;

@RestController

public class UserController {
    @GetMapping ("/welcome")

    public String welcome() {
        return "Welcome to Spring Security 6";
    }

}
```

If we enter the right username and password, we will get the "Welcome to Spring Security 6" message as shown in Figure 3-5.

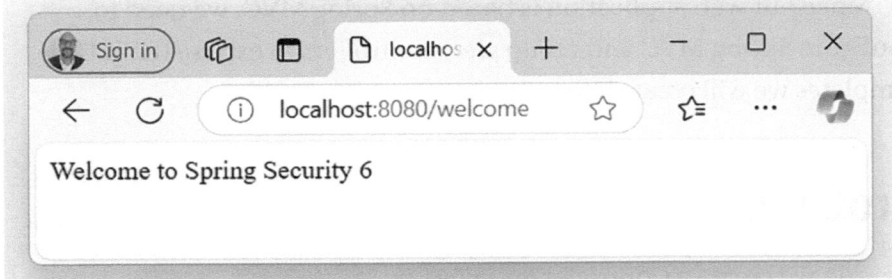

Figure 3-5. *Successful login message*

Let's add now some more logic to our code.

First of all, let's have a look at the new pom.xml file generated when we created the new Spring Boot 3 and Spring Security 6 project, as shown in Listing 3-2.

Listing 3-2. pom.xml file

```
<?xml version="1.0" encoding="UTF-8"?>
<project xmlns="http://maven.apache.org/POM/4.0.0"
xmlns:xsi="http://www.w3.org/2001/XMLSchema-instance"
    xsi:schemaLocation="http://maven.apache.org/POM/4.0.0
    https://maven.apache.org/xsd/maven-4.0.0.xsd">
    <modelVersion>4.0.0</modelVersion>
    <parent>
        <groupId>org.springframework.boot</groupId>
        <artifactId>spring-boot-starter-parent</artifactId>
        <version>3.3.5</version>
        <relativePath/> <!-- lookup parent from repository -->
    </parent>
    <groupId>com.apress</groupId>
    <artifactId>pss01_Security</artifactId>
    <version>0.0.1-SNAPSHOT</version>
    <name>pss01_Security</name>
```

```
<description>Demo project for Spring Boot and spring
Security v6</description>
<url/>
<licenses>
    <license/>
</licenses>
<developers>
    <developer/>
</developers>
<scm>
    <connection/>
    <developerConnection/>
    <tag/>
    <url/>
</scm>
<properties>
    <java.version>23</java.version>
</properties>
<dependencies>
    <dependency>
        <groupId>org.springframework.boot</groupId>
        <artifactId>spring-boot-starter-security</artifactId>
    </dependency>
    <dependency>
        <groupId>org.springframework.boot</groupId>
        <artifactId>spring-boot-starter-web</artifactId>
    </dependency>

    <dependency>
        <groupId>org.springframework.boot</groupId>
        <artifactId>spring-boot-starter-test</artifactId>
        <scope>test</scope>
```

```
        </dependency>
        <dependency>
            <groupId>org.springframework.security</groupId>
            <artifactId>spring-security-test</artifactId>
            <scope>test</scope>
        </dependency>
    </dependencies>

    <build>
        <plugins>
            <plugin>
                <groupId>org.springframework.boot</groupId>
                <artifactId>spring-boot-maven-plugin</artifactId>
            </plugin>
        </plugins>
    </build>

</project>
```

As you can see, we use Thymeleaf which is a Java template engine that can be used for processing and creating HTML, XML, CSS, JavaScript, and plain text.

To activate Spring Security Web project configuration in your Maven Web Application, you need to configure a particular servlet filter that will take care of preprocessing and postprocessing the requests, as well as managing the required security constraints.

Problem

How do we create admin users to access some authenticated resource?

Solution

Let's define two users in our project, but only the "Admin" with the role "Admin" will be authorized to access the secured resource called "authenticated.html" in our project.

As a first step, please make sure that all the tools and directories are created as described previously.

Next, create the needed simple HTML files under a new project directory called src/main/resources/templates/.

Your project will utilize two html pages:

- welcome.html, which is the starting welcome web page of the project

- authenticated.html, which is the admin web page to access when the user successfully logs in

The welcome.html page is shown in Listing 3-3.

Listing 3-3. welcome.html

```
<!DOCTYPE html>
<html xmlns="http://www.w3.org/1999/xhtml" xmlns:th="https://
www.thymeleaf.org">
<html lang="en">
<head>
    <meta http-equiv="Content-Type" content="text/html;
    charset=ISO-8859-1">
    <title>Spring Security 6 authentication example!</title>
</head>
<body>

<div th:if="${param.error}">
    Invalid username and password.
</div>
```

```
<div th:if="${param.logout}">
    You have been logged out.
</div>

<h2>Welcome to Spring Security 6 authentication example!</h2>

<p>Click <a th:href="@{/authenticated}">here</a> to get
authenticated!</p>

</body>
</html>
```

The welcome.html page will only display a welcoming message and provide the link to the authenticated page, /authenticated.

Let's now create the authenticated.html page as shown in Listing 3-4.

Listing 3-4. authenticated.html

```
<!DOCTYPE html>
<html xmlns="http://www.w3.org/1999/xhtml" xmlns:th="https://
www.thymeleaf.org"
      xmlns:sec="https://www.thymeleaf.org/thymeleaf-extras-
      springsecurity6">
<head>
    <title>Spring Security 6 authentication example</title>
</head>
<body>
<h2>Welcome to Spring Security 6 authentication example!</h2>
<h2 th:inline="text">You are an authenticated user: <span
th:remove="tag" sec:authentication="name">thymeleaf</
span>!</h2>

<p>click <a th:href="@{/logout}">here</a> to logout!!</p>

</body>
</html>
```

Next, you need to define the Java classes needed for your example. Under the package controller:

- UserController

Under the package configuration:

- SecurityConfiguration

Let's create the two Java packages where your Java classes will be located:

- package com.apress.pss01_security.configuration
- package com.apress.pss01_security.controller;

Problem

In Spring Security, how is the UserController Java class built?

Solution

Let's create the UserController Java class under the package com.apress. pss01_security.controller, as shown in Listing 3-5.

Listing 3-5. UserController Java class

```
package com.apress.pss01_security.controller;

import org.springframework.stereotype.Controller;
import org.springframework.ui.ModelMap;
import org.springframework.web.bind.annotation.GetMapping;

@Controller
public class UserController {
```

```
@GetMapping("/")
public String homePage() {
    return "welcome";
}

@GetMapping("/welcome")
public String welcomePage() {
    return "welcome";
}

@GetMapping ("/authenticated")
public String AuthenticatedPage() {
    return "authenticated";
}

@GetMapping ("/logout")
public String logoutPage() {
return "redirect:/welcome";
}
```

}

Note that, for the purposes of web security, it doesn't really matter if you use a Spring MVC controller, like you do here, or if you use simple servlets, as you did in Chapter 3, or for that matter, if you use any other servlet-based framework for developing your application. Remember that, at the core, the web part of Spring Security basically attaches itself to the standard Java servlet filter architecture. So if your application uses servlets and filters, you can leverage Spring Security's web support.

Problem

What are the most common HTTP mapping annotations based on @RequestMapping?

Solution

Since Spring Framework 4.3, there are some new HTTP mapping annotations based on @RequestMapping:

- @GetMapping

- @PostMapping

- @PutMapping

- @DeleteMapping

- @PatchMapping

For instance, @GetMapping is a specialized version of the @RequestMapping annotation, which will act as a shortcut for @RequestMapping(method = RequestMethod.GET). @GetMapping annotates methods to handle the HTTP GET requests matched with a certain given URI expression.

As we all developers well know, MVC applications aren't service oriented, which means that there will be a view resolver which will render the final views based on data received from the controller.

RESTful applications are designed to be service oriented and return raw data, which is generally JSON/XML, and since these applications don't do any view rendering, there are no view resolvers, and the controller is typically expected to send data directly via the HTTP response.

The UserController Java class simply, via Spring MVC, will

1. Intercept any incoming request

2. Convert the payload of the request to the internal structure of the data

3. Send the data to Model for any needed further processing

4. Get processed data from the Model, and advance it to the View for rendering

So, for instance, in our example, the "UserController Java class" will

1. Return a view named "welcome."

2. The view resolver will try to resolve a page called "welcome.html" in the templates folder.

Problem

How does the "SecurityConfiguration" Java class work?

Solution

We already explained previously how to enable Spring Security v6 using the annotation named "@EnableWebSecurity" without using the WebSecurityConfigurerAdapter class and also introduced in that chapter the Java Spring Security configuration class named "SecurityConfiguration" which will utilize "@EnableWebSecurity" annotation, to help us to configure the Spring Security–related beans, such as WebSecurityConfigurer and SecurityFilterChain.

Here is what exactly our "SecurityConfiguration" will do in this example:

- Create two demo in-memory users via "UserDetailsService" named "user" and "admin" which will be authorized to access a secure resource of the project so that only user "Admin" can access the secured "authenticated" web resource.

- Use BCryptPasswordEncoder to encode the user passwords for added security.

- Configure the SecurityFilterChain bean with the username/password basic authentication mechanism to authenticate the users.

Listing 3-6 shows the SecurityConfiguration Java class.

Listing 3-6. SecurityConfiguration.java

```
package com.apress.pss01_security.configuration;

import org.springframework.context.annotation.Bean;
import org.springframework.context.annotation.Configuration;
import org.springframework.security.config.Customizer;
import org.springframework.security.config.annotation.web.
builders.HttpSecurity;
import org.springframework.security.config.annotation.web.
configuration.EnableWebSecurity;
import org.springframework.security.core.userdetails.User;
import org.springframework.security.core.userdetails.
UserDetails;
import org.springframework.security.core.userdetails.
UserDetailsService;
import org.springframework.security.crypto.bcrypt.
BCryptPasswordEncoder;
import org.springframework.security.crypto.password.
PasswordEncoder;
import org.springframework.security.provisioning.
InMemoryUserDetailsManager;
import org.springframework.security.web.SecurityFilterChain;

@Configuration
@EnableWebSecurity

public class SecurityConfiguration {

    @Bean
    public SecurityFilterChain filterChain1(HttpSecurity http)
    throws Exception {
        http
```

```
            .authorizeHttpRequests((authorize) -> authorize
                    .requestMatchers("/", "/welcome").
                    permitAll()
                    .requestMatchers("/authenticated").
                    hasRole("ADMIN")
                    .anyRequest().denyAll()

            )
            .csrf(Customizer.withDefaults())
            .formLogin(withDefaults())

            .logout((logout) -> logout
                    .logoutSuccessUrl("/welcome")
                    .invalidateHttpSession(true)
                    .permitAll()
            );

        return http.build();
    }

    @Bean
    public UserDetailsService userDetailsService(){

        UserDetails user = User.builder()
                .username("user")
                .password(passwordEncoder().
                encode("userpassw"))
                .roles("USER")
                .build();

        UserDetails admin = User.builder()
                .username("admin")
                .password(passwordEncoder().encode("adminpassw"))
                .roles("ADMIN")
                .build();
```

```
        return new InMemoryUserDetailsManager(user, admin);
    }

    @Bean
    public static PasswordEncoder passwordEncoder(){
        return new BCryptPasswordEncoder();
    }
}
```

Spring Security allows us to model our authorization at the request level. In our example, we are saying that page /welcome is permitted to all pages under /admin require one authority while all other pages simply require authentication.

By default, Spring Security requires that every request be authenticated. That said, any time you use an HttpSecurity instance, it's necessary to declare your authorization rules.

Whenever you have an HttpSecurity instance, you should at least do

```
http
    .authorizeHttpRequests((authorize) -> authorize
        .anyRequest().authenticated()
    )
```

So in our case:

- "/" and "/welcome" are permitted to all

- "/authenticated" page can only be accessed when presenting a usr with "role " Admin via the .hasRole("ADMIN") declaration

- .logout((logout) -> logout is permitted to all and in case it is utilized it will request the "welcome.html" page

All the info about http-requests can be found at spring doc web page:

```
https://docs.spring.io/spring-security/reference/servlet/
authorization/authorize-http-requests.html
```

Problem

What are the special URLs in Spring Security?

Solution

As we explained so far, you can see that Spring Security's support for web security defines a few preconfigured URLs for you to use in your application. These URLs get special treatment in the framework. The main ones are the following:

- /login: This is the URL that Spring Security uses to show the login form for the application. The framework will redirect to this URL when an authentication is needed but doesn't exist yet.

- /logout: This URL is used by the framework to log out the currently logged-in user, invalidating the corresponding session and SecurityContext.

From the previous URLs, the first thing that comes to mind is how to configure your own login form in the application and, in general, how to customize the login process instead of using the default one. That is what we'll do next.

Problem

What kind of HTTP filters can be used with Spring Security, and what are the most common?

Solution

Spring Security utilizes a lot of filters. In the case of the HTTP request filter, it will be used to

- Intercept the request

- Detect authentication (or absence of)

- Redirect to authentication entry point

- Pass the request to authorization service

- Send the request to the servlet or throw security exception

The most important Spring Security v6 filters are

- BasicAuthenticationFilter: If it finds a Basic Auth HTTP Header on the request, it tries to authenticate the user with the header's username and password.

- UsernamePasswordAuthenticationFilter: If it finds a username/password request parameter/POST body, it tries to authenticate the user with those values.

- DefaultLoginPageGeneratingFilter: It generates a default login page when enabling Spring Security unless we explicitly disable that feature.

- DefaultLogoutPageGeneratingFilter: It generates a logout page for us unless we explicitly disable that feature.

- FilterSecurityInterceptor: It does our authorization.

Let's learn more about some of the Spring Security v6 filters when using the URL /login.

Let's see what happens when incorrect or correct credentials are provided when logging in. When the browser is redirecting and asks for the URL /login, the following occurs:

- The process is the same as for the first request until it reaches the DefaultLoginPageGeneratingFilter. At this point, the filter detects that the request is for the URL /login and writes the login form's HTML data directly in the response object. Then the response is rendered.

Now try to log in with incorrect credentials.
Let's follow the request through the framework to see what happens:

- In the login form, type the username **admin** and the password **adminpassw**.

- When the form is submitted, the filters are activated again in the same order as before. This time, however, when the request arrives at the Username PasswordAuthenticationFilter, the filter checks whether the request is for the URL /login and sees that this is indeed the case. The filter extracts the username and password authentication information from the HTTP request parameters username and password, respectively. With this information, it creates the UsernamePasswordAuthenticationTok en Authentication object, which then sends it to the AuthenticationManager (or more exactly, its default implementation, ProviderManager) for authentication.

- The DaoAuthenticationProvider gets called from the ProviderManager with the Authentication object. The DaoAuthenticationProvider is an implementation of AuthenticationProvider, which uses a strategy of UserDetailsService to retrieve the

users from whichever storage they live in. With the
configuration you currently have, it will try to find a
user with the username of user using the configured
InMemoryUserDetailsManager (the implementation
of UserDetailsService that maintains an in-memory
user storage in a java.util.Map). Because there is
no user with this username, the provider throws a
UsernameNotFoundException exception.

- The provider itself catches this exception and converts
  it into a BadCredentialsException to hide the fact
  that there is no such user in the application; instead,
  it treats the error as a common username-password
  combination error.

- The exception is caught by the
  UsernamePasswordAuthenticationFilter. This
  filter delegates to an instance of an implementation
  of AuthenticationFailureHandler, which in
  turn decides to redirect the response to the URL
  /login?error. This way, the login form is shown again
  in the browser with an error message displayed.

You can see all the documentation on filters at https://docs.spring.
io/spring-security/reference/6.1-SNAPSHOT/servlet/architecture.
html#servlet-filters-review.

Restart the application, go back to the URL http:/localhost:8080/
welcome, which will trigger the login page, and type **admin** as the username
and **adminpassw** as the password in the form. Then click the Login button.

- The request follows the same filter journey as before.
  This time, InMemoryUserDetailsManager finds a
  user with the requested username and returns that
  to DaoAuthenticationProvider, which creates a
  successful Authentication object.

- After successful authentication, the
  UsernamePasswordAuthenticationFilter
  delegates to an instance of
  SavedRequestAwareAuthenticationSuccessHandler,
  which looks for the original requested URL (/
  authenticated) in the session and redirects the
  response to that URL.

When http://localhost:8080/authenticated is requested, the
request works its way through the filter chain as in the previous cases. This
time, though, you already have a fully authenticated entity in the system.
The request arrives in the FilterSecurityInterceptor.

- The FilterSecurityInterceptor receives an
  access request to the URL / authenticated. Then it
  recovers the necessary credentials to access that URL
  (ROLE_ADMIN).

- The AffirmativeBased access-decision manager gets
  called and in turn calls the RoleVoter voter. The voter
  evaluates the list of authorities of the authenticated
  entity and compares them with the required credentials
  to access the resource. Because the voter finds a match
  (ROLE_ADMIN is in both the Authentication authorities
  and the resource's config attributes), it votes with an
  ACCESS_GRANTED vote.

- The FilterSecurityInterceptor forwards the request
  to the next element in the request-handling chain,
  which in this case is Spring's DispatcherServlet.

- The request gets to the AdminController, which simply
  returns the authenticated page.

Problem

How do we build a customized login form in Spring Security?

Solution

Since v5, when you use Spring Security, the user authentication request to your application is done via the `http.authorizeRequests()` method.

When you configure the `http` element, via the `http.authorizeHttpRequests ()` method, as you did before, Spring Security takes care of setting up a default login and logout process for you, including a login URL, login form, default URL after login, and some other options. Basically, when Spring Security's context starts to load up, it will find that there is no custom login page URL configured, so it will assume the default one and create a new instance of `DefaultLoginPageGeneratingFilter` that will be added to the filter chain. As you saw before, this filter is the one that generates the login form for you.

If you want to configure your own form, you need to do the following tasks. The first thing is to tell the framework to replace the default handling with your own. You define the following element as a child of the `http.authorizeRequests()` method in the `SecurityConfiguration` Java file:

formLogin((form) -> form

This element tells Spring Security to change its default login-handling mechanism on startup. First, the `DefaultLoginPageGeneratingFilter` will no longer be instantiated. Let's try this first configuration out. With the new configuration in place, restart the application and try to access the URL `http://localhost:8080/ /authenticated`.

You get redirected to the URL `/login` and get a 404 HTTP error because you haven't defined any handler for this URL yet. This 404 page is shown in Figure 3-6.

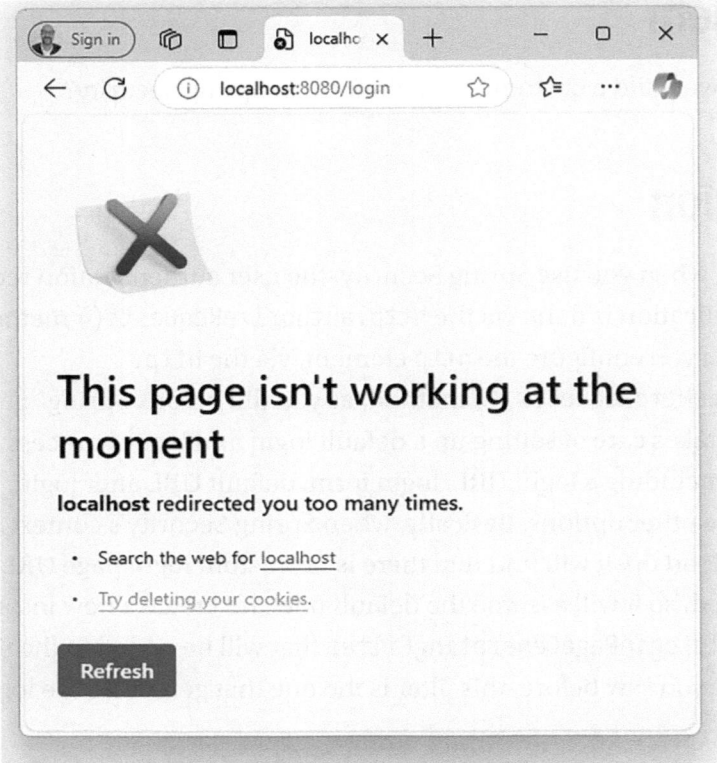

Figure 3-6. *Error 404 that appears when defining a new login handler page*

Let's add a login controller in the UserController as shown in Listing 3-7.

Listing 3-7. Login controller added to the UserController

```
@GetMapping("/login")
  public String loginPage() {
     return "login";
}
```

Next, add the following line to the SecurityConfiguration file:

```
formLogin((form) -> form
      .loginPage("/login")
      .permitAll()
)
```

Now create the login.html page from Listing 3-8 in the folder templates in your application.

Listing 3-8. Custom login.html

```
<!DOCTYPE html>
<html xmlns="http://www.w3.org/1999/xhtml" xmlns:th="https://
www.thymeleaf.org" lang="">
<head>
  <title>Spring Security Example </title>
</head>
<body>

<div th:if="${param.logout}">
  You have been logged out.
</div>

<h1>Spring Security v6 Custom Login Form</h1>
<h2>Login with Username and Password:</h2>
<form th:action="@{/login}" method="post">

  <div th:if="${param.error}">
    <p th:text="#{login.error}">Invalid username or
    password.</p>
  </div>

  <div><label> Username : <input type="text" name="username"
  required /> </label></div>
```

```
<div><label> Password: <input type="password" name="password"
required /> </label></div>
<div><input type="submit" value="Login"/></div>
</form>
</body>
</html>
```

In the authenticated.html file, replace the following line:

```
<p>Click <a th:href="@{/logout}">here</a> to logout!!</p>
```

with this:

```
<form th:action="@{/logout}" method="post">
    <input type="submit" value="Logout"/>
</form>
```

If you restart the application and again go to http://localhost:8080/ welcome, you should see the welcome page as shown in Figure 3-7.

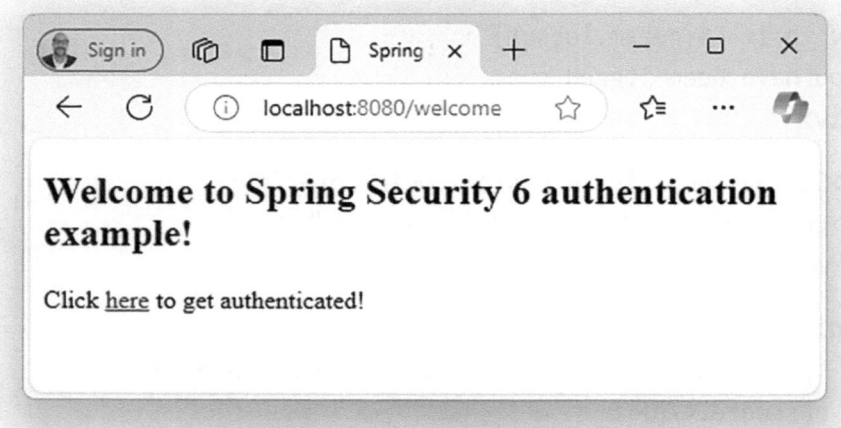

Figure 3-7. *Welcome web page*

When you click to authenticate, then the application goes to http:// localhost:8080/authenticated; you should see your new login form when you get redirected to the /login URL. The form is shown in Figures 3-8 and 3-9. If you type **admin** as username and **adminpassw** as password, you get access to the authenticated page, as you did before with the default login form.

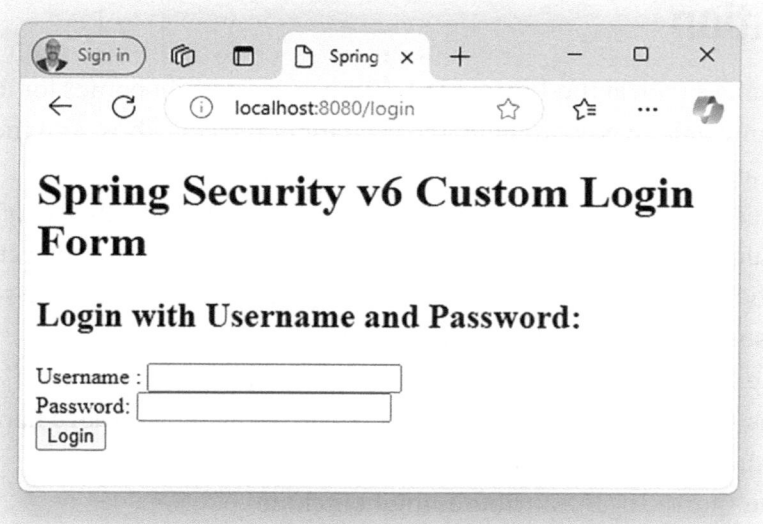

Figure 3-8. *Custom login form*

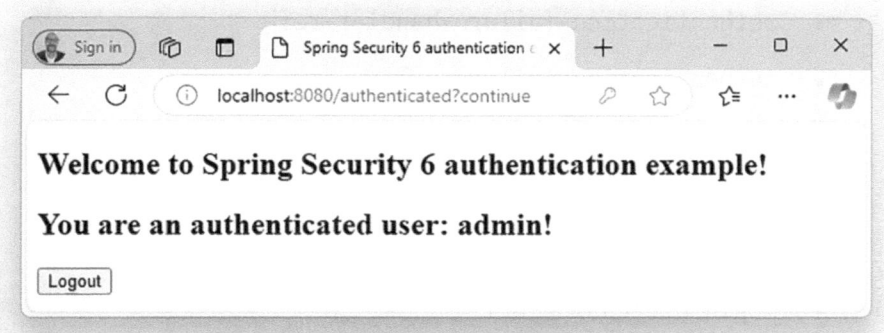

Figure 3-9. *Custom successful login form*

Just click "Logout" to log out the current user.

Problem

How do we build a customized error message in our web page?

Solution

If you take a look at the `login.html`, you can see certain names for the username field, password field, the remember me checkbox, and the action attribute of the form element.

These are not random names. Spring Security expects the use of these particular names in order to treat the authentication process correctly. Also, the form should use POST for sending the information to the server because this is required by the framework.

The element `<form-login>` supports many more configuration options, including changing the default `username` and `password` names for the authentication request parameters.

The `<form-login>` attributes might include

- `always-use-default-target`
- `authentication-details-source-ref`
- `authentication-failure-handler-ref`
- `authentication-failure-url`
- `authentication-success-handler-ref`
- `default-target-url`
- `login-page`
- `login-processing-url`
- `password-parameter`
- `username-parameter`

- authentication-success-forward-url

- authentication-failure-forward-url

Give this attribute the value /login. Then, in your login.html, add the content from Listing 3-9 just after the <body> tag.

Listing 3-9. Snippet showing an error in the login.jsp

```
<div th:if="${param.error}">
  <p th:text="#{login.error}">Invalid username or password.</p>
</div>
```

If you now restart the application and try to access the URL http:// localhost:8080/ /authenticated and use an incorrect username and password, you will get the login page again, but with the error message "Invalid username and password" shown at the top. Look at Figure 3-10 for the page you should be getting.

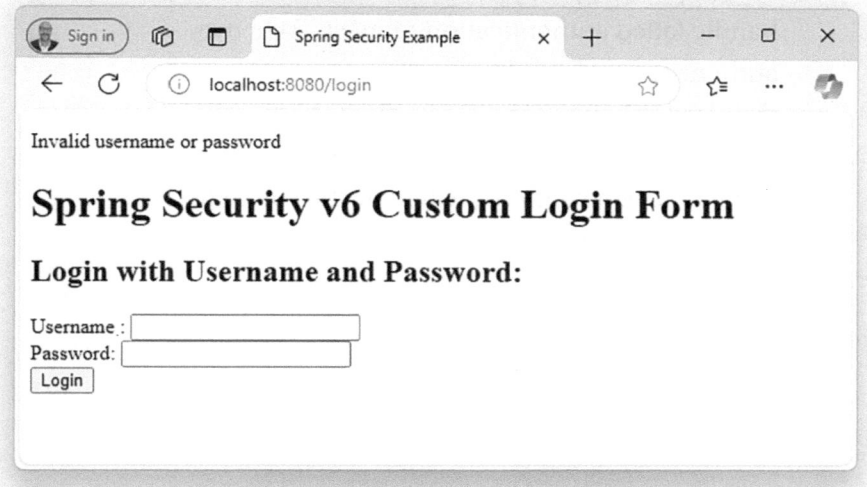

Figure 3-10. *A custom error shown in the custom form*

Note that this URL could be a different URL altogether, not related to the login URL at all. But the common pattern is to allow the user another attempt at logging in, showing them any errors.

- `authentication-success-handler-ref`: Reference to an `AuthenticationSuccessHandler` bean in the Spring application context. This bean is called upon successful authentication and should handle the next step after authentication, usually deciding the redirect destination in the application. A current implementation in the form of `SavedRequestAwareAuthenticationSuccessHandler` takes care of redirecting the logged-in user to the original requested URL after successful authentication.

- `authentication-failure-handler-ref`: Reference to an `AuthenticationFailureHandler` bean in the Spring application context. It is used to handle failed authentication requests. When an authentication fails, this handler gets called. A standard behavior for this handler is to present the login screen again or return a 401 HTTP status error. This behavior is provided by the concrete class `SimpleUrlAuthenticationFailureHandler`.

When authenticating a Spring Security application, there are three different interfaces to consider:

- Authentication Success Handler

- Authentication Failure Handler

- Access Denied Handler

Let's develop a simple example implementation of the
AuthenticationFailureHandler interface. It will simply return
a 500 status code when failing to authenticate. Create the class
CustomAuthenticationFailureHandler from Listing 3-10.

Listing 3-10. AuthenticationFailureHandler implementation for
ServerErrorFailureHandler

```
package com.apress.pss01_security.configuration;

import jakarta.servlet.http.HttpServletRequest;
import jakarta.servlet.http.HttpServletResponse;
import org.springframework.security.core.
AuthenticationException;
import org.springframework.security.web.authentication.
AuthenticationFailureHandler;

import java.io.IOException;

public class CustomAuthenticationFailureHandler implements
AuthenticationFailureHandler {

    @Override
    public void onAuthenticationFailure(HttpServlet
    Request request, HttpServletResponse response,
    AuthenticationException exception)
            throws IOException {
        response.sendError(500);
    }
}
```

Then, add to the SecurityConfiguration class file the following:

```
.formLogin((form) -> form
        .loginPage("/login")
        .defaultSuccessUrl("/authenticated")
```

```
    .permitAll()
    .failureHandler(authenticationFailureHandler())
```

And the new bean:

```
@Bean
public AuthenticationFailureHandler
authenticationFailureHandler() {
    return new CustomAuthenticationFailureHandler();
}
```

Restart the application, go to http://localhost:8080/authenticated, use a random username and password, and click the Submit button. You should get a 500 error in the browser.

Finally, in Listing 3-11, you see the entire "SecurityConfiguration" Java class.

Listing 3-11. SecurityConfiguration.java

```
package com.apress.pss01_security.configuration;

import org.springframework.context.MessageSource;
import org.springframework.context.annotation.Bean;
import org.springframework.context.annotation.Configuration;
import org.springframework.context.support.
ReloadableResourceBundleMessageSource;
import org.springframework.security.config.Customizer;
import org.springframework.security.config.annotation.web.
builders.HttpSecurity;
import org.springframework.security.config.annotation.web.
configuration.EnableWebSecurity;
import org.springframework.security.config.http.
SessionCreationPolicy;
import org.springframework.security.core.userdetails.User;
```

```
import org.springframework.security.core.userdetails.
UserDetails;
import org.springframework.security.core.userdetails.
UserDetailsService;
import org.springframework.security.crypto.bcrypt.
BCryptPasswordEncoder;
import org.springframework.security.crypto.password.
PasswordEncoder;
import org.springframework.security.provisioning.
InMemoryUserDetailsManager;
import org.springframework.security.web.SecurityFilterChain;
import org.springframework.security.web.access.
AccessDeniedHandler;
import org.springframework.security.web.authentication.
AuthenticationFailureHandler;
import org.springframework.security.web.authentication.
AuthenticationSuccessHandler;
import org.springframework.security.web.authentication.www.
DigestAuthenticationEntryPoint;
import org.springframework.security.web.authentication.www.
DigestAuthenticationFilter;
import org.springframework.security.web.session.
HttpSessionEventPublisher;

import static org.springframework.security.config.
Customizer.withDefaults;

@Configuration
@EnableWebSecurity

public class SecurityConfiguration {
```

```
@Bean
public SecurityFilterChain filterChain1(HttpSecurity http)
throws Exception {
    http
                .authorizeHttpRequests((authorize) -> authorize
                        .requestMatchers("/", "/welcome").
                        permitAll()
                        .requestMatchers("/authenticated").
                        hasRole("ADMIN")
                        .requestMatchers("/customError").
                        permitAll()
                        .anyRequest().denyAll()
                )

                .csrf(withDefaults())
                .formLogin(withDefaults())

                .sessionManagement(session -> session
                        .sessionCreationPolicy(SessionCreation
                        Policy.ALWAYS)
                        .maximumSessions(1))

                // using customized login html page
                .formLogin((form) -> form
                        .loginPage("/login")
                        .defaultSuccessUrl("/authenticated")
                        .failureUrl("/login?error=true")
                        .failureHandler(authenticationFailure
                        Handler())
                        .permitAll()
                )

                .logout((logout) -> logout
```

```
                .logoutSuccessUrl("/welcome")
                .deleteCookies("JSESSIONID")
                .invalidateHttpSession(true)
                .permitAll()
        );

        return http.build();
    }

    @Bean
    public MessageSource messageSource() {
        ReloadableResourceBundleMessageSource messageSource =
        new ReloadableResourceBundleMessageSource();
        messageSource.setBasename("classpath:messages");
        messageSource.setDefaultEncoding("UTF-8");
        return messageSource;
    }

    @Bean
    public AuthenticationFailureHandler
    authenticationFailureHandler() {
        return new CustomAuthenticationFailureHandler();
    }

    @Bean
    public HttpSessionEventPublisher
    httpSessionEventPublisher() {
        return new HttpSessionEventPublisher();
    }

    @Bean
    public UserDetailsService userDetailsService(){

        UserDetails user = User.builder()
```

```
                    .username("user")
                    .password(passwordEncoder().encode("userpassw"))
                    .roles("USER")
                    .build();

        UserDetails admin = User.builder()
                    .username("admin")
                    .password(passwordEncoder().encode("adminpassw"))
                    .roles("ADMIN")
                    .build();

        return new InMemoryUserDetailsManager(user, admin);
    }

    @Bean
    public static PasswordEncoder passwordEncoder(){
        return new BCryptPasswordEncoder();
    }
}
```

The final project will look like Figure 3-11.

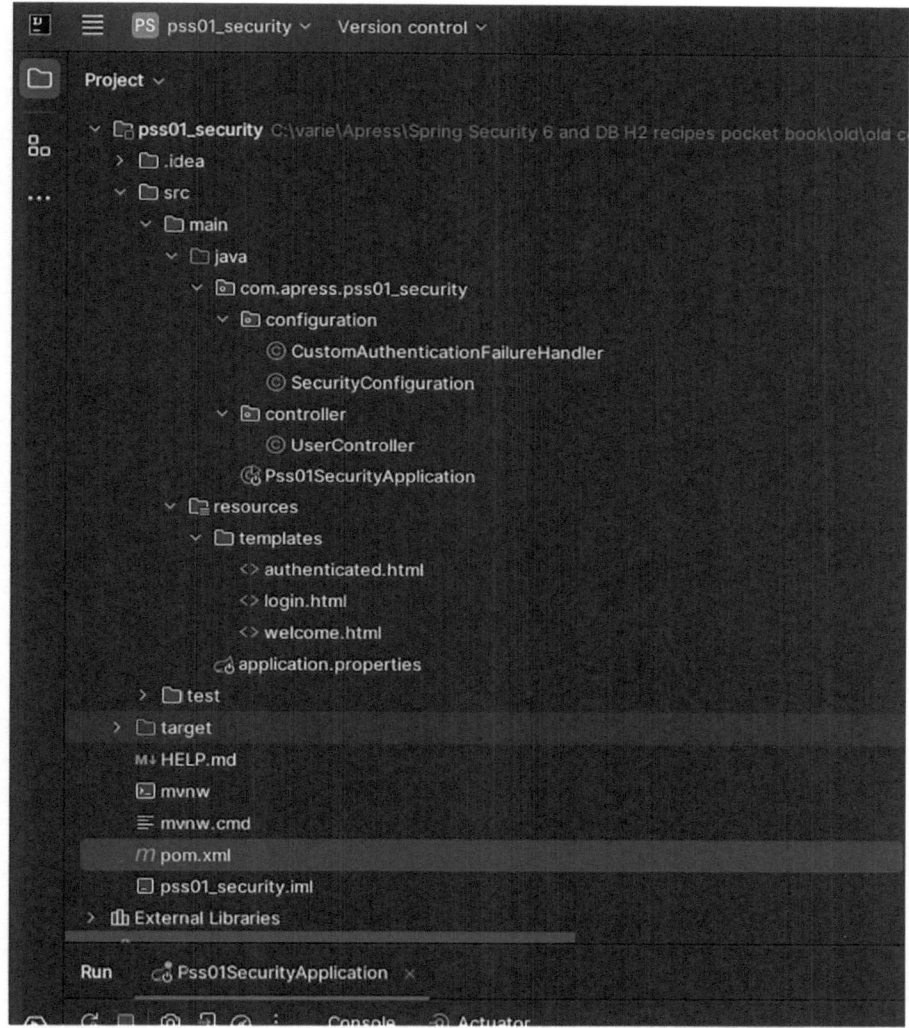

Figure 3-11. *Final project window*

Our final pom.xml file is shown in Listing 3-12.

Listing 3-12. Final pom.xml file

```xml
<?xml version="1.0" encoding="UTF-8"?>
<project xmlns="http://maven.apache.org/POM/4.0.0"
xmlns:xsi="http://www.w3.org/2001/XMLSchema-instance"
    xsi:schemaLocation="http://maven.apache.org/POM/4.0.0
    https://maven.apache.org/xsd/maven-4.0.0.xsd">
    <modelVersion>4.0.0</modelVersion>
    <parent>
        <groupId>org.springframework.boot</groupId>
        <artifactId>spring-boot-starter-parent</artifactId>
        <version>3.3.5</version>
        <relativePath/> <!-- lookup parent from repository -->
    </parent>
    <groupId>com.apress</groupId>
    <artifactId>pss01_security</artifactId>
    <version>0.0.1-SNAPSHOT</version>
    <name>pss01_security</name>
    <description>Spring Security demo</description>
    <properties>
        <java.version>23</java.version>
    </properties>
    <dependencies>
        <dependency>
            <groupId>org.springframework.boot</groupId>
            <artifactId>spring-boot-starter-thymeleaf</artifactId>
        </dependency>
        <dependency>
            <groupId>org.thymeleaf.extras</groupId>
            <artifactId>thymeleaf-extras-springsecurity6
            </artifactId>
        </dependency>
```

```xml
    <dependency>
        <groupId>org.springframework.boot</groupId>
        <artifactId>spring-boot-starter-security</artifactId>
    </dependency>
    <dependency>
        <groupId>org.springframework.boot</groupId>
        <artifactId>spring-boot-starter-web</artifactId>
    </dependency>

    <dependency>
        <groupId>org.springframework.boot</groupId>
        <artifactId>spring-boot-starter-test</artifactId>
        <scope>test</scope>
    </dependency>
    <dependency>
        <groupId>org.springframework.security</groupId>
        <artifactId>spring-security-test</artifactId>
        <scope>test</scope>
    </dependency>
    <dependency>
    <groupId>org.thymeleaf.extras</groupId>
    <artifactId>thymeleaf-extras-springsecurity6
    </artifactId>
    <version>3.1.1.RELEASE</version>
    </dependency>
  </dependencies>

</project>
```

Summary

In this chapter, we covered how to build a Java Web Application using Spring Security 6 in Spring Boot 3 Initializr. You learned in detail the inner work of the security filter chain and the different metadata options at your disposal to define security constraints in your application.

Finally, we learned how to build a customized Spring Security login form.

In the next chapter, we will cover how to add an H2 Database to Spring Boot with Spring Security and JDBC authentication.

CHAPTER 4

Spring Data JDBC and H2 Database

Spring Security's flexibility shines through its support for various authentication mechanisms that can be seamlessly integrated. It's designed with a highly modular, pluggable architecture, allowing different components to be added to the framework effortlessly. In the authentication layer, this flexibility is provided by an abstraction layer, primarily represented by the AuthenticationProvider interface, as well as by specific security servlet filters and user detail services that support the process.

Spring Security v6 supports many different authentication mechanisms, including

- Database
- LDAP
- X.509
- OAuth 2/OpenID Connect 1.0
- WebSockets
- JSON Web Token (JWT)
- JAAS
- CAS

© Massimo Nardone 2025
M. Nardone, *Spring Security 6 Recipes*, Apress Pocket Guides,
https://doi.org/10.1007/979-8-8688-1297-2_4

In this chapter, we will only cover how to add the H2 Database to Spring Boot with Spring Security and JDBC authentication.

Let's see how to create a new Spring Boot project with Spring Security, Spring Data JDBC, and H2 Database.

Problem

How do we create a new Spring Boot project with Spring Security, Spring Data JDBC, and H2 Database?

Solution

Let's go to start.spring.io and create a new project, shown in Figure 4-1, with the following settings:

- Build Tool: Maven

- Language: Java

- Packaging: Jar

- Java Version: 23

Next, add the following dependencies:

- Web

- Spring Security

- Spring Data JDBC

- H2 Database

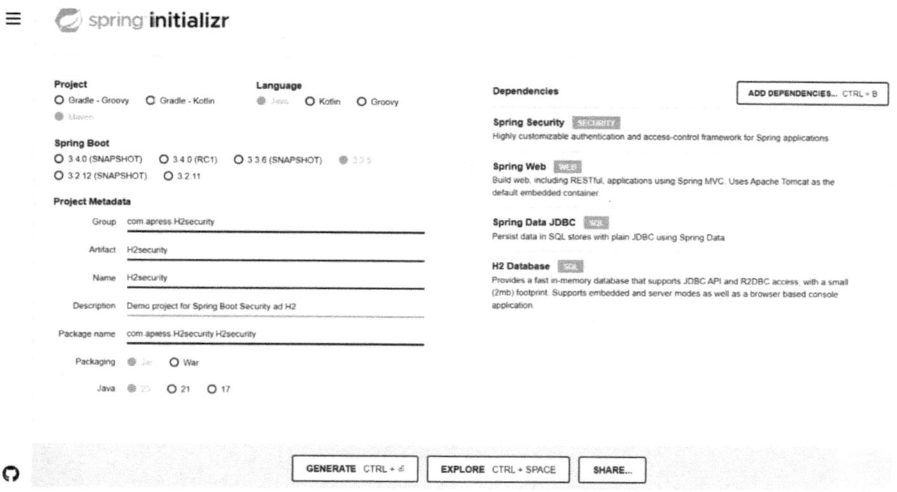

≡   🌱 spring initializr

Project
○ Gradle - Groovy   ○ Gradle - Kotlin
● Maven

Language
● Java   ○ Kotlin   ○ Groovy

Spring Boot
○ 3.4.0 (SNAPSHOT)   ○ 3.4.0 (RC1)   ○ 3.3.6 (SNAPSHOT)   ● 3.3.5
○ 3.2.12 (SNAPSHOT)   ○ 3.2.11

Project Metadata
Group   com.apress.H2security
Artifact   H2security
Name   H2security
Description Demo project for Spring Boot Security ad H2
Package name com.apess.H2security.H2security
Packaging   ● Jar   ○ War
Java   ● 23   ○ 21   ○ 17

Dependencies   [ADD DEPENDENCIES... CTRL + B]

Spring Security SECURITY
Highly customizable authentication and access-control framework for Spring applications

Spring Web WEB
Build web, including RESTful, applications using Spring MVC. Uses Apache Tomcat as the default embedded container.

Spring Data JDBC SQL
Persist data in SQL stores with plain JDBC using Spring Data

H2 Database SQL
Provides a fast in-memory database that supports JDBC API and R2DBC access, with a small (2mb) footprint. Supports embedded and server modes as well as a browser based console application.

[GENERATE CTRL + ↵]   [EXPLORE CTRL + SPACE]   [SHARE...]

Figure 4-1. *Creating a new JDBS and H2 DB project*

Generate the project and unzip it on your machine.

The new project will look as shown in Figure 4-2.

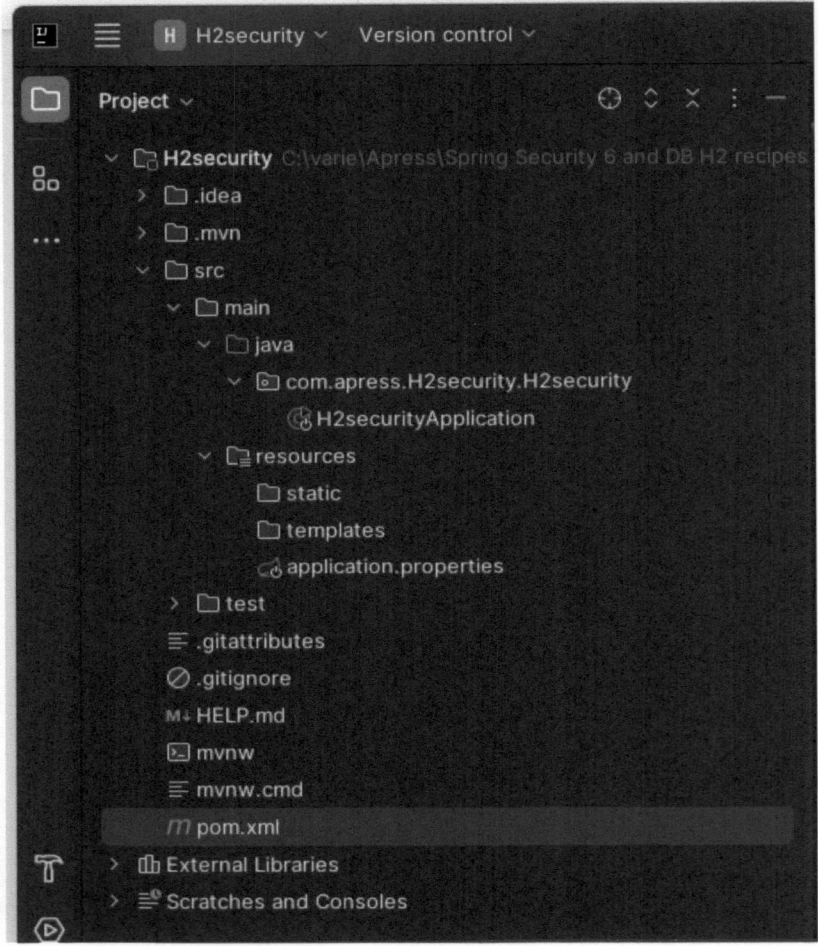

Figure 4-2. *New JDBS and H2 DB project*

Problem

How do we enable H2 in our application.properties file?

Solution

In order to use the H2 in-memory database console, we must enable and configure it in our application.properties file as follows.

Add the following lines to the application.properties file:

```
spring.h2.console.enabled=true
spring.datasource.name=securitydb
spring.datasource.url=jdbc:h2:mem:securitydb
spring.jpa.database-platform=org.hibernate.dialect.H2Dialect
spring.datasource.driverClassName=org.h2.Driver
```

These lines will tell our web application to enable the console, the name of the DB we wish to use, the datasource URL and driver class, as well as the Spring JPA DB platform.

Problem

What are the new needed Maven dependencies to be added automatically to the pom.xml file?

Solution

Here are the new JDBC and H2 Maven dependencies we will find automatically in the pom.xml file as we selected them when we generated the new project:

```
<dependency>
    <groupId>org.springframework.boot</groupId>
    <artifactId>spring-boot-starter-data-jdbc</artifactIc>
</dependency>
```

```
<dependency>
    <groupId>com.h2database</groupId>
    <artifactId>h2</artifactId>
    <scope>runtime</scope>
</dependency>
```

Listing 4-1 will show the new pom.xml file after generating this new project.

Listing 4-1. Updated pom.xml file

```
<?xml version="1.0" encoding="UTF-8"?>
<project xmlns="http://maven.apache.org/POM/4.0.0"
xmlns:xsi="http://www.w3.org/2001/XMLSchema-instance"
    xsi:schemaLocation="http://maven.apache.org/POM/4.0.0
    https://maven.apache.org/xsd/maven-4.0.0.xsd">
    <modelVersion>4.0.0</modelVersion>
    <parent>
        <groupId>org.springframework.boot</groupId>
        <artifactId>spring-boot-starter-parent</artifactId>
        <version>3.3.5</version>
        <relativePath/> <!-- lookup parent from repository -->
    </parent>
    <groupId>com.apress.H2security</groupId>
    <artifactId>H2security</artifactId>
    <version>0.0.1-SNAPSHOT</version>
    <name>H2security</name>
    <description>Demo project for Spring Boot Security ad H2
    </description>
    <url/>
    <licenses>
        <license/>
    </licenses>
```

```
<developers>
    <developer/>
</developers>
<scm>
    <connection/>
    <developerConnection/>
    <tag/>
    <url/>
</scm>
<properties>
    <java.version>23</java.version>
</properties>
<dependencies>
    <dependency>
        <groupId>org.springframework.boot</groupId>
        <artifactId>spring-boot-starter-data-jdbc</artifactId>
    </dependency>
    <dependency>
        <groupId>org.springframework.boot</groupId>
        <artifactId>spring-boot-starter-security</artifactId>
    </dependency>
    <dependency>
        <groupId>org.springframework.boot</groupId>
        <artifactId>spring-boot-starter-web</artifactId>
    </dependency>

    <dependency>
        <groupId>com.h2database</groupId>
        <artifactId>h2</artifactId>
        <scope>runtime</scope>
    </dependency>
```

```
    <dependency>
        <groupId>org.springframework.boot</groupId>
        <artifactId>spring-boot-starter-test</artifactId>
        <scope>test</scope>
    </dependency>
    <dependency>
        <groupId>org.springframework.security</groupId>
        <artifactId>spring-security-test</artifactId>
        <scope>test</scope>
    </dependency>
</dependencies>

<build>
    <plugins>
        <plugin>
            <groupId>org.springframework.boot</groupId>
            <artifactId>spring-boot-maven-plugin</artifactId>
        </plugin>
    </plugins>
</build>

</project>
```

Let's create some Java classes and HTML files to be used in our project.

Problem

How do we create and configure HTML files for our Spring Security project?

Solution

Let's create two simple HTML files under a new project directory called src/main/resources/templates/.

Your project will utilize two html pages:

- welcome.html, which is the starting welcome web page of the project

- authenticated.html, which is the admin web page to access when the user successfully logs in

The welcome.html page is shown in Listing 4-2.

Listing 4-2. welcome.html

```
<!DOCTYPE html>
<html xmlns="http://www.w3.org/1999/xhtml" xmlns:th="https://
www.thymeleaf.org">
<html lang="en">
<head>
    <meta http-equiv="Content-Type" content="text/html;
    charset=ISO-8859-1">
    <title>Spring Security 6 authentication example!</title>
</head>
<body>

<div th:if="${param.error}">
    Invalid username and password.
</div>
<div th:if="${param.logout}">
    You have been logged out.
</div>
```

```
<h2>Welcome to Spring Security 6 authentication example!</h2>

<p>Click <a th:href="@{/authenticated}">here</a> to get
authenticated!</p>

</body>
</html>
```

The `welcome.html` page will only display a welcoming message and provide the link to the authenticated page, `/authenticated`.

Problem

How do we create an HTML page to get a user authenticated in H2?

Solution

Let's create the `authenticated.html` page as shown in Listing 4-3.

Listing 4-3. authenticated.html

```
<!DOCTYPE html>
<html xmlns="http://www.w3.org/1999/xhtml" xmlns:th="https://
www.thymeleaf.org"
      xmlns:sec="https://www.thymeleaf.org/thymeleaf-extras-
      springsecurity6">
<head>
    <title>Spring Security 6 authentication example</title>
</head>
<body>
<h2>Welcome to Spring Security 6 authentication example!</h2>
<h2 th:inline="text">You are an authenticated user: <span
th:remove="tag" sec:authentication="name">thymeleaf</span>!</h2>
```

```
<p>click <a th:href="@{/logout}">here</a> to logout!!</p>
<form th:action="@{/h2-console}" method="post">
    <input type="submit" value="check the h2-console"/>
</form>

</body>
</html>
```

This will simply create a new button once the user is authenticated to open the H2 console and check the databases updated using our example.

The Java class named UserController will remain the same as in Chapter 3.

Problem

How do we update our Java code to use the H2 embedded database?

Solution

Let's update now the SecurityConfiguration Java class file we created in Chapter 3 to use the H2 embedded database as shown in Listing 4-4.

Listing 4-4. Updated SecurityConfiguration Java class

```
package com.apress.H2security.H2security.configuration;

import org.springframework.context.annotation.Bean;
import org.springframework.context.annotation.Configuration;
import org.springframework.jdbc.datasource.embedded.
EmbeddedDatabase;
import org.springframework.jdbc.datasource.embedded.
EmbeddedDatabaseBuilder;
```

```
import org.springframework.jdbc.datasource.embedded.
EmbeddedDatabaseType;
import org.springframework.security.config.Customizer;
import org.springframework.security.config.annotation.web.
builders.HttpSecurity;
import org.springframework.security.config.annotation.web.
configuration.EnableWebSecurity;
import org.springframework.security.core.userdetails.User;
import org.springframework.security.core.userdetails.UserDetails;
import org.springframework.security.core.userdetails.jdbc.
JdbcDaoImpl;
import org.springframework.security.crypto.bcrypt.
BCryptPasswordEncoder;
import org.springframework.security.crypto.password.
PasswordEncoder;
import org.springframework.security.provisioning.
JdbcUserDetailsManager;
import org.springframework.security.web.SecurityFilterChain;
import org.springframework.security.web.util.matcher.
AntPathRequestMatcher;

import javax.sql.DataSource;

@Configuration
@EnableWebSecurity

public class SecurityConfiguration {

    @Bean
    public SecurityFilterChain filterChain1(HttpSecurity http)
    throws Exception {
        http

            .csrf(csrf -> csrf.ignoringRequestMatchers("/h2-
            console/**"))
```

```
        .authorizeHttpRequests((authorize) -> authorize
                .requestMatchers("/", "/welcome").
                permitAll()
                //.requestMatchers("/authenticated").
                hasRole("ADMIN")
                .requestMatchers("/authenticated").
                hasAnyRole("USER", "ADMIN")
                .requestMatchers(AntPathRequest
                Matcher.antMatcher("/h2-console/**")).
                permitAll()
        )

        .csrf(csrf -> csrf
                .ignoringRequestMatchers(AntPathRequest
                Matcher.antMatcher("/h2-console/**")))

        .formLogin(Customizer.withDefaults())

        .headers(headers -> headers.disable())

        .logout((logout) -> logout
                .logoutSuccessUrl("/welcome")
                .deleteCookies("JSESSIONID")
                .invalidateHttpSession(true)
                .permitAll()
        );

    return http.build();
}

@Bean
EmbeddedDatabase datasource() {
    return new EmbeddedDatabaseBuilder()
            .setName("securitydb")
```

```java
            .setType(EmbeddedDatabaseType.H2)
            .addScript(JdbcDaoImpl.DEFAULT_USER_SCHEMA_DDL_
            LOCATION)
            .build();
}

@Bean
JdbcUserDetailsManager users(DataSource dataSource,
PasswordEncoder encoder) {
    UserDetails user = User.builder()
            .username("user")
            .password(encoder.encode("userpassw"))
            .roles("USER")
            .build();
    UserDetails admin = User.builder()
            .username("admin")
            .password(encoder.encode("adminpassw"))
            .roles("ADMIN")
            .build();
    JdbcUserDetailsManager jdbcUserDetailsManager = new
    JdbcUserDetailsManager(dataSource);
    jdbcUserDetailsManager.createUser(user);
    jdbcUserDetailsManager.createUser(admin);
    return jdbcUserDetailsManager;
}

@Bean
public static PasswordEncoder passwordEncoder(){
    return new BCryptPasswordEncoder();
}
}
```

Let's analyze this new Java class.

The PasswordEncoder bean will stay the same as per previous examples.

Spring Security's JdbcDaoImpl implements UserDetailsService to provide support for username- and password-based authentication that is retrieved by using JDBC. JdbcUserDetailsManager extends JdbcDaoImpl to provide management of UserDetails through the UserDetailsManager interface. UserDetails-based authentication is used by Spring Security when it is configured to accept a username/password for authentication.

Spring Security provides default queries for JDBC-based authentication, which of course we can adjust the schema to match any customizations to the queries and the database dialect we use.

Problem

How do the JdbcDaoImpl required tables look like?

Solution

JdbcDaoImpl requires tables to load the password, account status (enabled or disabled), and a list of authorities (roles) for the user. The default schema is also exposed as a classpath resource named org/springframework/security/core/userdetails/jdbc/users.ddl, which is provided in the following listing:

```
create table users(
    username varchar_ignorecase(50) not null primary key,
    password varchar_ignorecase(500) not null,
    enabled boolean not null
);
```

```
create table authorities (
      username varchar_ignorecase(50) not null,
      authority varchar_ignorecase(50) not null,
      constraint fk_authorities_users foreign key(username)
      references users(username)
);
```

Before we configure JdbcUserDetailsManager, we must create a DataSource, and in our example, we set up an embedded DataSource that is initialized with the default user schema via the EmbeddedDatabase datasource bean created to build a new H2 Database, in our case named "securitydb," using the preconfigured JDBC Dao Implementation default user DDL via the line

```
"DJdbcDaoImpl.DEFAULT_USER_SCHEMA_DDL_LOCATION"
@Bean
EmbeddedDatabase datasource() {
    return new EmbeddedDatabaseBuilder()
            .setName("securitydb")
            .setType(EmbeddedDatabaseType.H2)
            .addScript(JdbcDaoImpl.DEFAULT_USER_SCHEMA_DDL_
            LOCATION)
            .build();
```

The next step will be creating the JdbcUserDetailsManager bean as described in Listing 4-5.

Listing 4-5. JdbcUserDetailsManager Java bean

```
@Bean
JdbcUserDetailsManager users(DataSource dataSource,
PasswordEncoder encoder) {
    UserDetails user = User.builder()
            .username("user")
```

```
            .password(encoder.encode("userpassw"))
            .roles("USER")
            .build();
    UserDetails admin = User.builder()
            .username("admin")
            .password(encoder.encode("adminpassw"))
            .roles("ADMIN")
            .build();
    JdbcUserDetailsManager jdbcUserDetailsManager = new
    JdbcUserDetailsManager(dataSource);
    jdbcUserDetailsManager.createUser(user);
    jdbcUserDetailsManager.createUser(admin);
    return jdbcUserDetailsManager;
}
```

In our example, we will create two users needed to access the authenticated resource such as "user/userpassw" and "admin/ adminpassw."

Our last bean will be, as usual, the SecurityFilterChain bean as shown in Listing 4-6.

Listing 4-6. SecurityFilterChain Java bean

```
@Bean
public SecurityFilterChain filterChain1(HttpSecurity http)
throws Exception {
    http

            .authorizeHttpRequests((authorize) -> authorize
                    .requestMatchers("/", "/welcome").
                    permitAll()
                    .requestMatchers("/authenticated").
                    hasAnyRole("USER", "ADMIN")
```

```
                    .requestMatchers(AntPathRequestMatcher.
                    antMatcher("/h2-console/**")).permitAll()
            )

            .csrf(csrf -> csrf
                    .ignoringRequestMatchers(AntPathRequest
                    Matcher.antMatcher("/h2-console/**")))

            .formLogin(Customizer.withDefaults())

            .headers(headers -> headers.disable())

            .logout((logout) -> logout
                    .logoutSuccessUrl("/welcome")
                    .deleteCookies("JSESSIONID")
                    .invalidateHttpSession(true)
                    .permitAll()
            );

    return http.build();
}
```

In this bean, first of all, we create two "requestMatchers":

- .requestMatchers("/", "/welcome").permitAll() to permit all to access "/" and "welcome" pages

- .requestMatchers("/authenticated").
  hasAnyRole("USER", "ADMIN") to permit the user and admin to access the authenticated page

- .requestMatchers(AntPathRequestMatcher.ant
  Matcher("/h2-console/**")).permitAll() to permit to access the H2 console

Since our Spring Boot project uses Spring Security and we have the class that is annotated with @EnableWebSecurity annotation, we must disable the HTTP Header Frame Options; add the following to the configure() method of that class.

The frame options are necessary to prevent a browser from loading your HTML page in an <iframe> or <frame> tag. To enable the H2 console page to load, you need to disable this option with this line:

```
.headers(headers -> headers.disable())
```

The line `.csrf(csrf -> csrf`

```
.ignoringRequestMatchers(AntPathRequestMatcher.antMatcher("/h2-
console/**")))
```

will allow ignoring the RequestMatchers for the H2 console path "/h2-console/**".

Build and run our Spring Boot application and open the URL http://localhost:8080/welcome in our browser window and authenticate with user "user/userpassw" or "admin/adminpassw," as shown, for example, in Figures 4-3 and 4-4.

Welcome to Spring Security 6 authentication example!

Click here to get authenticated!

Figure 4-3. *welcome.html page*

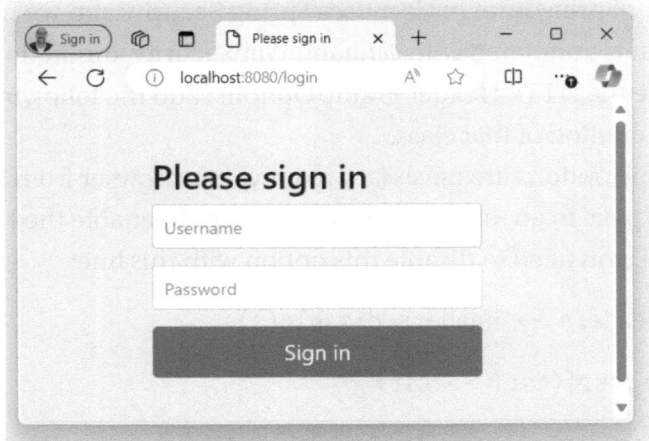

Figure 4-4. *Login page*

As in the previous example, if authenticated we will access the
authenticated.html page, which this time will not only inform that admin
is an authenticated user but also provide us a "check the h2-console
button" as shown in Figure 4-5.

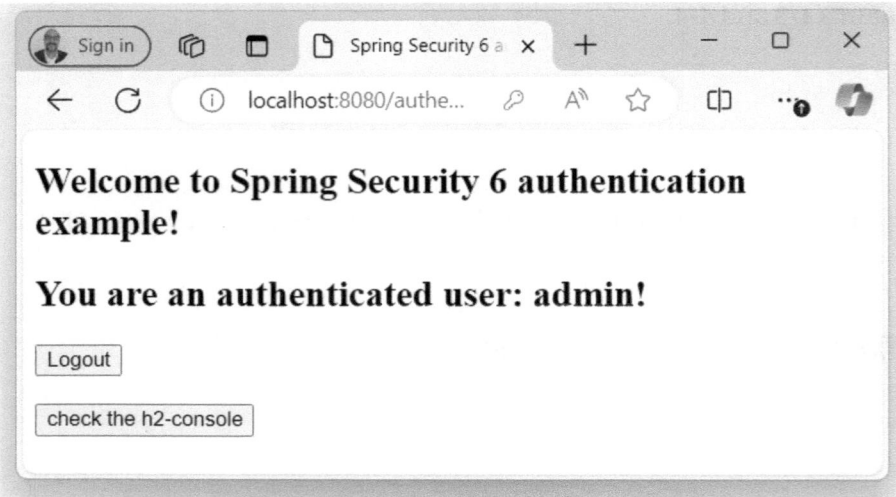

Figure 4-5. *authenticated.html page*

Problem

How do we open and configure the H2 console?

Solution

We open the H2 console when we click the "check the h2-console" button to log in to the H2 console as shown in Figure 4-6.

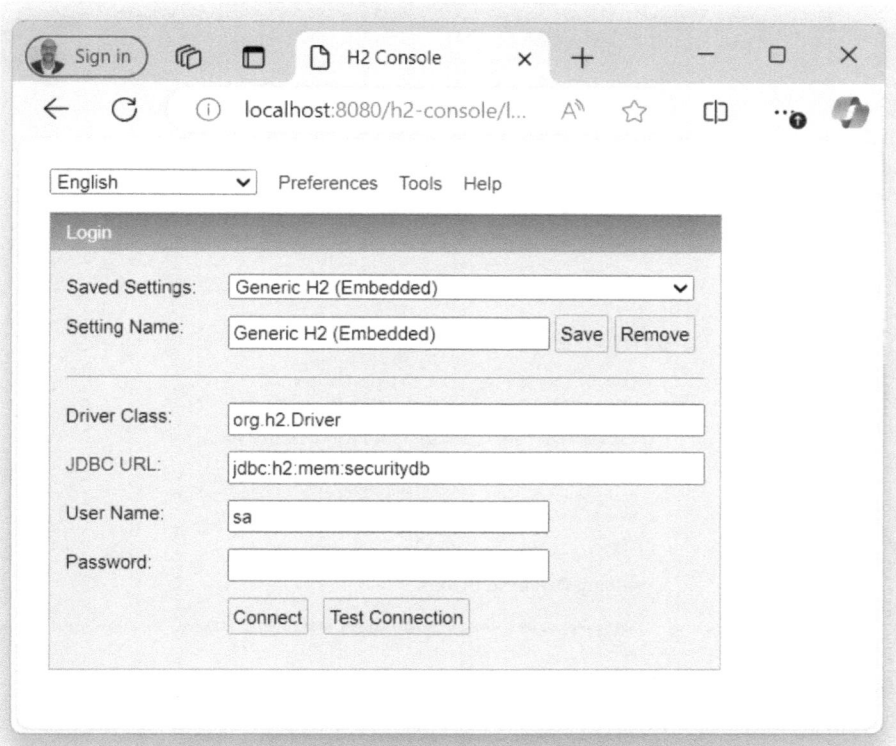

Figure 4-6. *H2 login console page*

Let's connect now to the H2 and discover the content as shown in Figure 4-7.

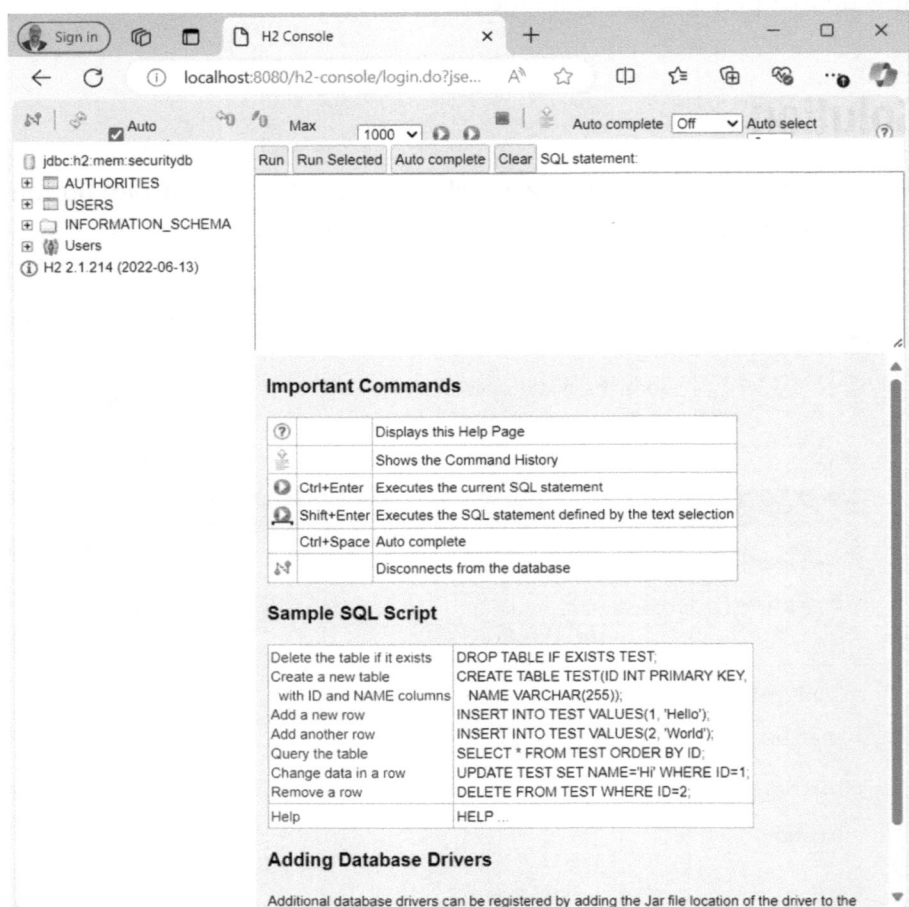

Figure 4-7. *H2 console page with securitydb DB tables*

As you will see, the H2 console will include the two tables used for this example via JDBC authentication, such as authorities and users.

Problem

How do we run SQL scripts against the securitydb database to see the content of the tables?

Solution

When running the SQL script SELECT * FROM AUTHORITIES, the result will be shown in Figure 4-8.

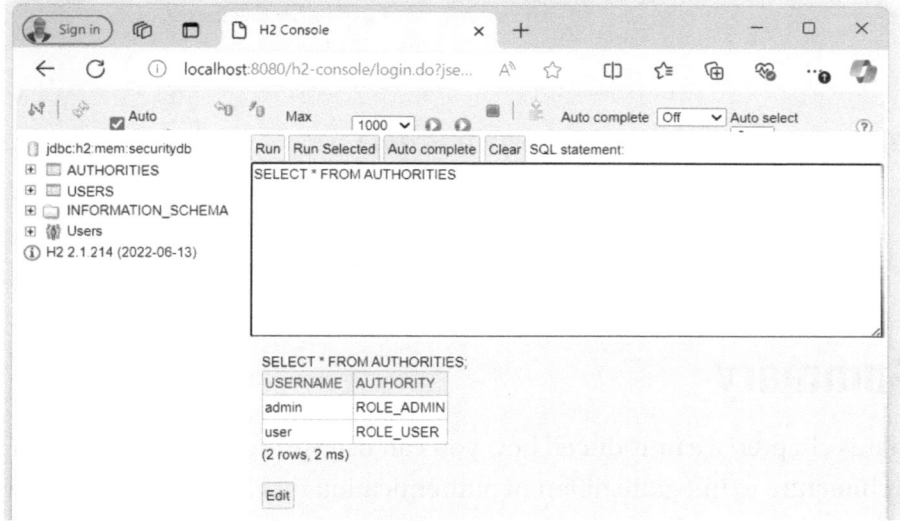

Figure 4-8. *H2 authorities table script outcome*

So we have two new authorities, "admin/ROLE_ADMIN" and "user/ROLE_USER," in our authorities DB.

When running the SQL script SELECT * FROM USERS, the result will be shown in Figure 4-9.

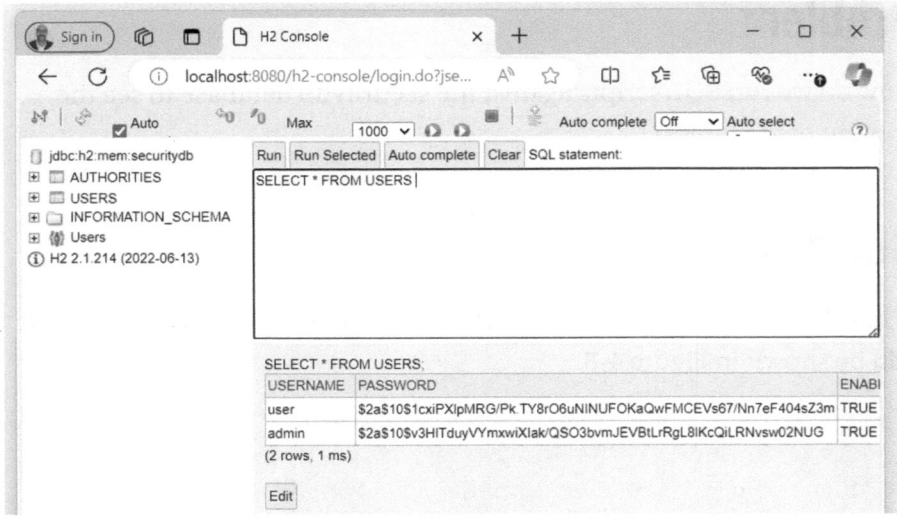

Figure 4-9. *H2 users table script outcome*

We will have two new enabled users, "user/userpassw" and "admin/adminpassw," to be used to authenticate our example.

Summary

In this chapter, we introduced how you can use Spring Security's modular architecture to integrate different authentication mechanisms with relative ease, and then we focused and explained how to authenticate your users against the H2 Database.

This chapter focused on the H2 Database and Spring JDBC, but of course as per our introduction, you can use many different authentication providers like LDAP, X.509, OAuth 2/OpenID Connect 1.0, JSON Web Token (JWT), etc.